PRAISE FOR I PROMISE NO

National Outdoor Book Award 2014 Winner

"With wonderful turns of phrase, a keen observant eye, and self-deprecating style, Storey is a consummate story teller. In the end, we come to know her as someone with a ticklish sense of humor and a willing sufferer with a heart of gold."
—Judges' review, *National Outdoor Book Awards*

". . . . an enjoyable and frank memoir that will appeal to those who have taken or want to take similar journeys, whether hiking or of the heart."
—*Library Journal*

"For anyone who has ever wondered if they have what it takes to push her boundaries, to attempt an endeavor the magnitude of the Pacific Crest Trail, this book will inspire."
—*Women's Adventure*

"*I Promise Not to Suffer* by Gail Storey is a true adventure memoir. . . . [Storey] explains how the experience changed her marriage, and how it changed them as individuals, eventually giving her insight she would not have found otherwise."
—Peter Greenberg, Travel Editor, *CBS News*

"Storey is refreshingly honest . . . at once humorous and sensitive. Woven among the accounts of harrowing trail mishaps and setbacks, as well as the celebrations of hard-won mileage ticked off and delightful and odd friends gained, it all makes for a strong sales pitch to anyone with half a foot in a boot toward taking on this daunting trek—not to mention that their suffering turns out to be quite the delightful read."
—*The Denver Post*

"Some have called Gail Storey the Nora Ephron of the wilderness. With her own unique wit, Storey shares Ephron's commitment to creating and tending a long, nourishing marriage. *I Promise Not to Suffer* is a portrait of a union that does not fray or break under pressure but is forged, toughened, and tenderized."
—Sara Davidson, author of *Leap!, Loose Change,* and *The December Project*

"In perfect indecorous fashion, [Gail Storey] claws up rocky mountainsides, sweats sticky-stinky across deserts, postholes through snowfield mush—all the while grappling for balance, not to drown in roiling creeks or deep-water matters of the heart. From her quest to blossom into the consummate trekking partner, she emerges, most dearly, as an unabashed sister to us all, and definitely a woman-of-the-wild."
—Kathleen Meyer, author of *How to Shit in the Woods*

"Ultimately, though, this is a love story. That's why, when Gail eventually leaves the trail and Porter continues on without her, the trail name he is given by other PCT hikers is 'Porter-and-Gail.' The story of Porter-and-Gail is one of passion and survival, a story that demonstrates how to pair yourself with another person in this world, through good times and bad."
—*The Daily Camera* (Boulder, Colorado)

"For the reader, though, the journey is not so much a linear undertaking marked mile by mile on a map, as it is an emotional journey—taking us into the depths of our own lives subtly and gracefully as Gail navigates the emotional terrain of woman, wife, partner, and daughter."
—*Female First*

"At times humorous, but always heartwarming, *I Promise Not to Suffer* lends credence to the belief that immersion in nature is healing and uplifting, purifying and spiritual. Only those who have gone forth and discovered it themselves can truly attest to this, but writers such as Storey allow glimpses into the sacred places of their experienced communion with the wild and with themselves."
—*Summit Daily News* (Colorado)

"If you think it's challenging to hike the Pacific Crest Trail solo, a feat author Cheryl Strayed describes so well in her bestselling book *Wild*, try it with your spouse. Gail Storey has given us another PCT gem."
—*North Shore Book Notes* (Gloucester, Massachusetts)

GAIL D. STOREY

I PROMISE NOT TO SUFFER

A FOOL FOR LOVE HIKES THE PACIFIC CREST TRAIL

THE MOUNTAINEERS BOOKS

THE MOUNTAINEERS BOOKS
is the nonprofit publishing arm of The Mountaineers, an organization
founded in 1906 and dedicated to the exploration, preservation, and
enjoyment of outdoor and wilderness areas.

1001 SW Klickitat Way, Suite 201, Seattle, WA 98134

Distributed in the United Kingdom by Cordee, www.cordee.co.uk
Manufactured in the United States of America

Copy Editor: Kim Runciman
Book Design and Illustrations: Heidi Smets Graphic Design
Cover photo composite by Heidi Smets. Trail photo © Tami Asars; skirt and legs
    © Veer; boots © Getty Images.
Author photo © Dana Rogers
Map on page 6: Porter Storey

The author gratefully acknowledges the editor of *Pilgrimage* magazine, in which tl
excerpted piece "Wind" appeared.

Library of Congress Cataloging-in-Publication Data

Storey, Gail Donohue.
  I promise not to suffer : a fool for love hikes the Pacific Crest Trail / Gail D. Store
Barbara Savage Memorial Award Winner.—First edition.
    pages cm
  Includes index.
  ISBN 978-1-59485-745-4 (pbk) — ISBN 978-1-59485-746-1 (ebook) (print)
1. Hiking—Pacific Crest Trail. 2. Pacific Crest Trail. 3. Storey, Gail Donohue—
Travel—Pacific Crest Trail. I. Title.
  GV199.42.P3S76 2013
  917.79—dc23

♻ Printed on 100% recycled paper
ISBN (paperback): 978-1-59485-745-4
ISBN (ebook): 978-1-59485-746-1

For Porter Storey, MD FACP FAAHPM,
Executive Vice President of the American Academy
of Hospice and Palliative Medicine (a.k.a. my husband)

CONTENTS

GRATITUDE

THE JOURNEY FROM SUN-SCORCHED, snow-soaked, tear-stained journal pages to a completed book is as long as the Pacific Crest Trail. First, thank you to those whose help was crucial to our survival while we were on the trail: Colleen Sweeney, who shipped us our resupplies; Jan and Bill Pollard, who rescued Porter from a weather-torn detour; Randy Turnbow and Martha Rice, whose kindness and cabin were a refuge; and Marcia Gerhardt, who brought her sewing machine as close to a trailhead as she could to mend a shredded tarp.

A new washing machine to Jeff and Donna L-Rod Saufley and a lifetime supply of taco salad fixin's to Terrie and Joe Anderson, for your warm hospitality when we needed it most, and wings to all the trail angels whose jugs of water kept us from dying of dehydration. Thanks to those whose guidebooks and shared wisdom proved indispensable: Yogi (Jackie McDonnell); Ben Schifrin, Jeffrey P. Schaffer, Thomas Winnett, Ruby Johnson Jenkins, and Andy Selters; Benedict "Gentle Ben" Go; and Leslie C. Croot. To the Pacific Crest Trail Association, 2,663 miles of thank-yous. We would have been lost, literally, without you.

Raucous thanks to my rockin' writing group: Julene Bair, Elisabeth Hyde, Lisa Jones, and Marilyn Krysl, for bringing your extraordinary literary talents, not to mention champagne and dinner, to the table. Were it not for you, well, let's not go there. Thanks also to discerning readers of the manuscript Jacqueline Damian, Margi Fox, Emily Fox Gordon, Janis Hallowell, Vicki Lindner, Jan Pollard, Connie Shaw, and Priscilla Stuckey. To Boulder Media Women, thank you for your support and irrepressible joie de vivre.

Many, many thanks to my agent, Ellen Levine, and to my editor, Kate Rogers, and her fabulous colleagues at The Mountaineers

Books. I'm grateful to Larry Savage for the Barbara Savage *Miles from Nowhere* Memorial Award.

Thank you, Tom and Sheila Pearson, Richard Efird, and all you other thru-hikers for your friendship and courage. A bowl of ramen noodles to the celebrity dog, whose name was changed at his request. Most of all, thank you, Porter, for loving me through the ferociously deep interior of the wilderness.

I NEVER MUCH CARED FOR NATURE

I NEVER MUCH CARED FOR NATURE, or rather, thought it okay as long as it stayed outside.

"Should we turn back?" I shouted, but my husband, Porter, couldn't hear me above the wind.

All morning we had sweated up the baked southwestern slopes of California's San Felipe Hills, through agave, cactus, and cholla, until the temperature plummeted thirty degrees.

Pelted by cold rain, we struggled with freezing fingers to dig out our warmest clothes, wet before we got them on. Porter had cut out the backs of our raincoats and sewed in nylon panels to cover our packs too, but wind drove in rain from beneath.

"In case I forget," he said, "these modified raincoats did not perform."

Sleet bit our faces and froze in his beard. At each round on the outward turn of a switchback, my coat filled like a spinnaker. Icy gusts pushed me to the edge of the gorge. I clung to the side of the mountain.

This was the late-winter, early-spring storm hikers dreaded. Our only hope was that our body heat from the struggle up and over the ridge top would ward off the hypothermia that chills the body's core. Each year, hikers freeze to death in the mountains under just these conditions. The cold reaches your brain and you lose what judgment you have left.

For five hours we sloshed up, down, and around the mountain's switchbacks in our wet socks and shoes, our freezing hands gripping our trekking poles. Finally, in the dark, we scrambled down into Barrel Spring to camp. We had hoped for a shelter of live oaks, but stumbled and bumped into each other under dripping trees. As soon as we set up one side of our tiny tarp, Porter insisted I crawl under it while he staked the other in the wind.

"Sweetheart," he bellowed, "get in the sleeping bag."

I knocked down our half-raised tarp dragging in our wet gear. He slipped in a deep puddle and we collapsed together into a soggy heap. He staggered up to shelter us as best he could under the seven-and-a-half-ounce nylon handkerchief we had instead of a real tent, too heavy in his expert opinion.

We lay on our bellies. Thunder shook the ground beneath us. Lightning flared in the blackness, cold rain pelted inches from our faces.

I was shocked into my own existence, born wet and confused on all fours on the muddy earth, deep in the loamy musk of it.

It had all started with Porter's crisis of meaning and purpose. It took us both by surprise, because he wasn't the crisis type. My whole life, on the other hand, had been a series of crises, one broken heart after another until I married him. Finally settled down, I looked forward to coffee together in the morning and wine with dinner, and in between a calm routine practicing the household and literary arts.

All of that changed when he came home from work one day, took off his doctor's coat, and began to cry. I sat down next to him on the sofa. I cried too, even though I didn't yet know what about. My arms around his big shaking shoulders, I waited. He took out his handkerchief and blew his nose. He was a man who still used starched white handkerchiefs.

"The hospice refused to pay for medications one of my inpatients needed," he said. He was the medical director of the premier nonprofit hospice in Houston. With a supportive board and compassionate staff, he had spent the last seventeen years growing it to a large home-care service with a freestanding inpatient building. But boards change, and the current one, now comprised of corporate executives, was all bottom-line.

"I understand the need to control costs," he went on, "but not at the expense of needed care."

"What did you do?" I asked.

"The patient's family didn't have the money," he said. "So I took out my checkbook."

"You did the right thing." But was he going to pay for all his patients' meds from then on? And I'd never seen him cry, much as he had probably felt like it, in all his years at the bedsides of dying people.

"I tried to work it out with the chairman of the board this afternoon," he said. "But in the end, he accepted my resignation."

I was flabbergasted, although most of the other staff members—doctors, nurses, social workers, and chaplains—had already left for similar reasons. Soon after, the hospice imploded and had to merge with another. Whatever—we were blasted out of the world we knew into one we were totally unprepared for.

Porter had loved to bicycle to work, his dress pants, shirt, and tie rolled in his bike bag. Once he'd called me from his office in a panic. "I left my pants at home," he said. I hopped in the car to bring them to him, while he hid behind his desk in his bike shorts. I made him chase me around his desk for them.

But now that he'd resigned from the hospice, he wanted to fulfill a lifelong dream: to bicycle 1,100 miles from Houston to Amicalola Falls, Georgia—the foot of the Appalachian Trail. Then he would hike the 2,100 miles of the Appalachian Trail north to Maine, bicycle from Maine back to Houston, bike from Houston to San Diego, hike the 2,663 miles of the Pacific Crest Trail north to Canada, and pedal home. He envisioned this route in the shape of a butterfly, and called it the Butterfly Route.

And while he was doing that, I'd be doing what?

I didn't give it much thought, because I couldn't imagine it happening. How would we afford it? But I was so relieved to see him excited about something that I just listened.

Long story very short, he took an interim job in a hospital, to set up a palliative care service bridging the gap between hospice and acute care, on the condition he could take time off to begin his Butterfly Route. I drove ahead and behind him in the car while he bicycled from Houston to Georgia, the lower right wing of the butterfly. Coordinating our respective whereabouts was so problematic, we drove home together and bought a tandem, so at least I'd know where he was. "That's a lot of 'quality time,'" a guy snickered when, two years later, Porter and I biked on our tandem the 2,400 miles from Houston to Maine, the butterfly's upper right wing. After seven weeks of biking from B&B to hostel to budget motel, we took apart our tandem and shipped it back to Houston, then the next day put on our packs to hike the Appalachian Trail south, the butterfly's outer right wing.

Profoundly unsuited to hiking and camping, I lasted only a few days on the AT. Rain chilled my sweat while I slogged pack-laden and blistered through bogs, sank in mud, and balanced precariously on mucky beaver dams. Fighting flies and mosquitoes, I dragged exhausted into a camp crowded with scruffy strangers, to help set up our tarp, filter water, and cook a mushy supper, only to have chipmunks try to grab the food from my mouth and mice run all over me. Mortified, I burst into tears and cried for the remainder of my outdoor adventure.

Porter continued south on the Appalachian Trail without me. We had rented out our house, so I patched together a parallel journey of my own, making my way by bus, train, and rental car to resupply him at remote trailheads. Nearly two months later, I went home. Something ominous was in the air. Having hiked seven hundred miles through Maine, New Hampshire, Vermont, Massachusetts, Connecticut, and New York, Porter left the Appalachian Trail and came home too, two days before the World Trade Center towers fell.

It would be two years before we resumed our Butterfly Route. The country had changed, and so had we. Porter postponed the rest of his Appalachian Trail hike from New York to Georgia so that together we could bicycle the butterfly's lower left wing. Our parents were aging, and my mother had survived her first fight with breast cancer. Older ourselves, with a deepening sense of our own mortality, we took off five weeks to bike 1,700 miles on our tandem from Houston to San Diego.

San Diego is near the southern terminus of the Pacific Crest Trail, the lower tip of the butterfly's outer left wing. We stood on the border of Mexico, one foot in one country, one in the other. I felt both the fear of the unknown and the lure of inner knowing.

All I knew for sure was that I loved him. I've never been able to explain it, even to myself. I came into his presence and never left. He's mountain-man buff, and at six feet two inches, just a head taller than I am, so our bodies fit perfectly. When he holds me, light-boned against his sculpted muscles, I know I'm being held. No matter how deeply I look into his gray-green eyes I never touch bottom. Ah, my soul said when we first met, aaahhh.

GETTING READY

ONLY A FEW HUNDRED HIKERS, mostly twenty-something men, start the Pacific Crest Trail at the Mexico/California border each year. About half make it all the way to Canada, hiking more than twenty miles a day over the steep mountains of Southern California, across the hot Mojave, up to the snow-covered peaks of the High Sierra, then fording icy rapids on their way to the lava fields of Oregon and the rainy forests of Washington. Several have died, others have been badly—even permanently—injured.

"We can do it in six months," Porter said one night over a kick-ass bottle of Malbec.

"Six months? Outside?"

"We'd have to start after the late-spring storms in southern California and finish before the early-fall blizzards in northern Washington," he said.

"Maybe *you* could hike for six months." Even he shouldn't attempt it. He was fifty-two and I was fifty-six. Fifty-six was the new thirty-six, but when would I get my turn to wallow moodily in menopause? Not to mention that on our cross-country bike trips, most nights we'd had a shower, café meal, and bed. To avoid camping, I'd pedaled up to ninety miles a day to a town.

"The problem is, I'd have to quit my job," he went on. "The hospital let me take off weeks at a time for our long-distance bike trips, but they'd have to replace me if I left for six months."

"The problem is, if you hike the PCT, I have to go too," I said. "And I'm not." Nature would get him over my dead body—I didn't want to worry about him all that time in the woods. I had worried enough when he hiked the AT.

"You don't have to come," he said, "but I know you'd really love it."

"You're going anyway? Whether I do or not?"

"I want to, but I won't if it freaks you out."

If he loved me enough to stay home, I loved him enough to let him hike the trail alone. But did I love him enough to fucking hike it with him?

"How will we pay the mortgage if we both stop working for six months?" I was a writer, and between book advances I freelanced and edited.

"We'll sell the house," he said.

I looked around the 1940s cottage we'd lived in since we married seventeen years ago. Porter, his four-year-old son, Philip, and I had house-hunted together. Porter liked one house because it was close to a gym, and I liked this one because it wasn't. "This house makes me feel happy and good," Philip had said to settle it. We'd done all of the work ourselves to lovingly restore it—sanding, insulating, painting. We'd jeopardized our marriage retiling the bathroom, the tiles came out so crooked. We took them all off, washed and dried them on the front lawn, and started over. But Porter is a do-it-yourselfer, and we had planned to live there until we died. "That's you in your eighties," I'd said, pointing out our window to Harry, our elderly next-door neighbor, high on a ladder in his cowboy boots.

Even if I hiked the PCT with Porter, which I had no business doing, wouldn't we come back to Houston afterwards? Much as I wouldn't want to worry about our house while we were gone for six months, I couldn't imagine parting with it.

Harry died in his bathtub, and his wife, Claudia, went to a nursing home. Soon after, I saw a real estate developer in Harry and Claudia's yard. As if I were someone else, someone I didn't even recognize, I asked whether he'd like to buy our house too.

The housing market was terrible; he would say no, and that would be that. He made an offer too good to refuse.

"I found a buyer for our house," I told Porter when he got home from work. I was horrified.

He was thrilled. His job as medical director of his hospice had ended, his interim job at a hospital was winding down, and he'd been shaken by the change in his role as father when Philip had gone off to college. To Porter, the easy sale of our house was yet another sign from the cosmos that now was the time to hike the trail.

I didn't like the idea of leaving our home and friends to hike until exhausted, then camp in the dirt. But I longed to be alone with Porter, far from the demands on our lives over the last seventeen years. Even more, I felt swept downstream by an irresistible momentum. I was caught up in it, my life seemed no longer my own. I couldn't go on this hike—it would be a nightmare. I was going, *and* it would be a nightmare. No, no, no! But yes.

Porter and I coped with our anxiety about the trip in different ways. We moved to a rented loft in Houston's downtown warehouse district, where he set up a kind of base camp. We put our bed in the loft living room so he could use the bedroom as a staging area for our six-month trek. He lined one wall with wire cubicles to sort the different types of jackets, shirts, pants, hats, gloves, socks, boots, and camping gear for the wildly varying weather of the Pacific Crest Trail, from hot desert to wind and rain, not to mention snow. He set up the sewing machine he'd inherited from his Aunt Noreen, and got busy making us an ultralight tarp and backpacks. He was a disciple of the ultralight gear king, Ray Jardine.

Meanwhile, I set about hosting dinner parties for friends we wouldn't see for six months, or ever again, if we died. I loved throwing dinner parties, complete with themed menus and party favors. No one could believe we were really going to hike the Pacific Crest Trail.

"You won't make her carry a pack on her little birdlike shoulders?" my friend Madeleine shrieked at Porter at one of our dinners.

I'm five feet seven inches and one hundred twenty-five pounds with barely 16 percent body fat.

"She has the perfect hiker's body from the waist down," he said.

I listened as they argued the merits of my long legs and "birthing" hips. Birthing hips? "That's enough," I said finally. "I'm too old to have a baby out there."

Porter got out the pack he was making for me, light enough for me to carry, with wide, well-padded straps for my bony shoulders and collarbone. Store-bought pack straps chafed and gave me blisters. But there was another problem, pack-wise—for a small-boned woman, I had big breasts.

"Where do my boobs go?" I asked when I tried it on. Straps placed wide apart slid off my shoulders. Narrowly placed, they crushed my breasts.

A lift-and-separate cross-my-heart version made Porter study the problem for more minutes than was called for.

"Doesn't anyone make a pack in a 32D?" I demanded.

Eventually, he came up with a padded band to connect the side straps across my upper chest, parallel to the strap across my hips. My breasts looked framed for a hikers' museum, but hey, it worked.

My women friends wondered how I would do my long brown hair, so thick they sometimes grabbed a handful to make sure it was real. I cut it short, since washings on the trail would be few and far between.

Our men friends worried about snakes, mountain lions, and bears. "I've watched a bear open a can of tuna with one swipe and suck out the contents in a lip-smacking second," one said. "And if a mountain lion comes after you, you're toast."

These were fears I couldn't relate to, unimaginable threats on an unimaginable trail. What I was really afraid of were my own unpredictable feelings. Would I cry and bail, as I had after my few horrible days on the Appalachian Trail?

What do you really want? I asked myself. To snuggle with Porter in the wilderness or fret alone at home in our cozy bed? One of the best parts of our marriage was waking up in the middle of the night and seeing for sure that the other was still on the planet. Not to mention our love life, although Porter began to stay up all night sewing our outdoor gear.

"You sew gear as a sublimation for sex," I told him.

"Sex," he said, "is a sublimation for people who can't sew their own equipment."

He made our sleeping quilt, a deep purple sleeping bag unzipped and sewed to a groundcloth, and named her Blueberry. He named our seven-ounce tarp Starshine, so thin we could see the stars through her. We'd leave at home our bigger tarp, Moonglow; our green one-person tarp, Spruce-Limb; and a gray sleeping bag called Charcoal.

I liked that he named all our gear. When you're out in the wilderness with no other people, your life-saving pieces of gear are your friends. But to him it was a matter of practicality to say, "Shall we take Blueberry or Vireo?" rather than, "Shall we take the purple Epic-cloth-covered eight-hundred-cubic-inch-per-ounce down-filled barrel-shaped two-pound full-zippered custom-made sleeping bag, or the black one-pound Pertex Quantum-covered no-zip tight mummy?"

He studied *Yogi's PCT Handbook,* by Jackie McDonnell, a loose-leaf binder packed with invaluable information on everything from gear and hiking tips to where to send resupply boxes. As soon as he'd made most of our gear, he switched to packing food. He ordered vast quantities of dehydrated everything: tomatoes, peas, corn, carrots, peppers, beans, beef, chicken, turkey, tofu, and texturized vegetable protein. Our food supplies took over the loft kitchen and dining areas. Noodles, nuts, chocolate, soup packets, and seasonings littered our dining room table.

The logistics of putting together twenty-five resupply boxes of food to ship to wilderness outposts over six months was mind-boggling, even for multitaskers like us. I tried to think of it as planning a series of bucolic brunches, picnic luncheons, and pastoral suppers.

"This is so complex, figuring quantities and portions," I said. "The top of my head's blowing off."

"Just fill these twenty-five plastic bags with rice," he said. "Then fill twenty-five sandwich bags with coffee, cocoa, and sugar."

"Why pack and ship resupply boxes instead of shopping as we go?"

"That works only for those fast enough to get to a real grocery store when they run out of food," he said.

Some hikers overplan—dehydrate food and pack for every meal only to find that one month into the six, they're sick of the sameness of their food. Still others, such as vegans and diabetics, have to plan minutely to eat what they need. A few hikers subsist on army rations. We would pack a variety of staples, then supplement from the town supermarkets—fresh bread, hard cheese, denatured alcohol or Heet for our camp stove. In town, we'd make up for deficiencies in ice cream and wine, gorging and getting blasted.

In our spare time, such as it was, we trained. We put on our packs, gradually increasing the weight, and hiked a few miles to the Texas Medical Center. Porter went to work at the hospital, and I sneaked into a coffee shop for a venti peppermint café mocha and a chocolate doughnut.

I wobbled home, full of primal doubt. What made me think I could hike all those miles? I'd been born with bowed legs, and wore a brace as a child—a bar to which my baby shoes were fastened. I didn't walk until I was past two, and throughout my childhood didn't trust my skinny legs to run or even jump rope. But at thirteen, I learned to dance. Even financially strapped as she was, my mother drove me on Thursday evenings to Katherine Dixon's ballroom dance class and waited outside while I struggled to learn the cha-cha, waltz, rock-a-conga. For the first time, my legs and feet began to seem part of my body. Dancing became for me what hiking was for Porter.

So I also trained by going to Jazzercise. My hips hurt, my knees hurt, I hurt all over from our training hikes, but I loved to dance. And I did yoga. I stood on my head a lot, although it remained to be seen how that would help me on the Pacific Crest Trail.

But mainly, I prepared emotionally. I struggled to deal with my fear by ordering my thoughts and feelings.

I made a mental list of reasons to hike the PCT: I wanted to have Porter even more to myself than I had on our bike trips, just the two of us out on the trail. I wanted to share the adventure of a lifetime with him, to understand what drew him to the wilderness, but also to know the power of the wilderness for myself. I was having my two-thirds-life crisis; I wanted to get ready for the last third of my life in a big way. When would I have another chance like this—to burn off the dross of my life and be consumed by nature? What the hell was nature, anyway?

It was futile, trying to impose logic on a movement of the heart. Porter's longing to hike the PCT also came from the heart, even as he tried to prepare logistically. But our approaches to the logistics differed. He looked ahead, to what the trip would require in terms of gear, food, and training, where I battened down the hatches of what we were leaving behind.

"I would've had time to make us a warmer sleeping bag," he said, "if you'd helped more instead of entertaining friends and typing lists."

"We'll miss our friends so much," I said. "And those lists will tell our families how to dispose of our stuff if we die. If we live, my lists of our accounts, insurance, and emergency contacts will keep our lives running while we're on the trail."

"Not that many people die. And your lists are overkill."

Overkill. I winced at the very word.

To fund our expedition, we sold a lot of our furniture, household items, and books, as if at our own estate sale. Hardest to part with was my fire-engine-red RX-7 sports car, with black leather bucket seats. Porter had given it to me one Valentine's Day.

I set up our bills for automatic payment. Our friend Colleen would handle our mail, and ship us our successive boxes of resupplies. Our friend Molly took our two tree-sized plants, one named Porter and the other Gail, to water sadly every day while we were dying of thirst in the high desert. Whether helpful, puzzled, or rueful, everyone seemed full of anticipatory grief.

LOST

IN SPITE OF ALL OUR ORGANIZING, we had too much left to do in the days, hours, and minutes before departure. I had vowed not to be frantic, but it was hopeless. Porter insisted on working at the hospital up to the afternoon before we left, while I sat at home at our dining room table making lists of everything we still had to do. I made lists in direct proportion to my terror, and the closer we got to leaving, the more terrified I was.

"Another list?" he asked when he got home.

"Couldn't we have had more of a cushion to get ready?" I asked. "You love to rush."

"You love to foot-drag." He nibbled the back of my neck.

At first we had planned to start with most other PCT hikers in late April at ADZPCTKO, the Annual Day Zero Pacific Crest Trail Kick Off party in Lake Morena, California. But being older and slower, we'd decided to start two weeks ahead of the pack to give ourselves lead-time.

It happened to be Good Friday. In my youth, I'd spent Good Friday walking the Stations of the Cross along the church walls. Now I paced our loft walls, lined with twenty-five cartons of food to be shipped to us one at a time by our friend Colleen. Porter and I drove ourselves crazy with last-minute packing, or rather de-packing, and paring down every possible ounce from our gear.

We worked through the night and collapsed into bed at 5:00 AM. We got up an hour later at 6:00 AM, and took a taxi to the airport. I couldn't believe we were leaving for six months with nothing but our backpacks. Mine had a base weight of eleven pounds, Porter's twelve, to which we would add food and water before we hit the trail and at every resupply stop after that.

In our matching wide-brimmed sunhats, long-sleeved shirts, and khaki hiking pants, we got on our flight to San Diego. Instead of the conventional pack frames Porter deemed too heavy, our packs had only a thin carbon-fiber rod to give them shape, like a spine. At home, we had removed these rods to check as luggage, along with our trekking poles, for airline security regulations.

"Where's my pack rod?" Porter asked at baggage claim, after we'd landed.

"It's not marked off our list." I'd have been smug if I hadn't been dismayed. "Someone must have left it at home."

His pack was as unwieldy as a sack of laundry without it. We took a taxi to a Wal-Mart, where he bought a fly rod as a substitute. He cut it to size with a hacksaw borrowed from Peanut, the PCT volunteer who would drive us an hour to the trailhead.

Peanut, an affable young composer whose business card read "Sonic Archaeology," had hiked short sections of the trail and planned to thru-hike it the following year. "Peanut" was his trailname. Nearly everyone gave up their old identity to become someone new in the wilderness.

Peanut and Porter rode in the car's front seat and talked about how much water we'd need to carry our first twenty miles.

Twenty miles to water? In the hundred-degree heat?

"You'll need about twenty quarts," Peanut said, "a quart an hour each, plus some for cooking supper and breakfast."

We clambered out of the car at the trailhead. Peanut filled our water bottles and soft-sided water bags. Porter loaded up with his ten quarts, but I could carry only three.

"Thanks," Porter said to Peanut. "We'll manage somehow."

Peanut waved goodbye and drove away.

The Pacific Crest Trail began near Campo, California, right on the border between Mexico and the United States. Border Patrol officers regularly searched the dusty road for footprints of illegal aliens, but now there was no one in sight. We touched the wall of rusty corrugated steel that divided the two countries, and for a moment I considered escaping to the other side.

Instead, I turned north to survey the rolling expanse of desert, sparsely dotted with cacti and brush. "Sure, a journey of 1,000 miles begins with a single step," I said, "but what about a journey of 2,663 miles?"

To "thru-hike" the Pacific Crest Trail in one continuous stretch, we'd have to hike an average of twenty miles a day, mostly up and down mountains. This average also had to take into account "zero days" of no trail mileage, in order to hike out of the wilderness, resupply in a remote town, and hike back to the trail. Some days we'd have to hike up to twenty-six miles to get to the next water. Other days, when the steep trail was hidden under snow in the High Sierra, ten miles would be an overwhelming challenge.

We walked up a knoll to sign the trail register at the border monument, a simple grouping of gray pillars inscribed "Southern Terminus, Pacific Crest National Scenic Trail."

It was 6 PM, the night before Easter. "Remember the Easter weekend you took me camping eighteen years ago?" I asked.

We were just dating then, and I had dressed for a date, with a purse and dressy shoes. I'd never been camping in my life. We went to an awful place in the Texas woods where, for the first time, I had to sleep on the ground. We pitched camp in the dark in what turned out to be a huge bed of poison ivy. We had our first real fight the next morning, referred to ever since as our Easter Morning Massacre. It was about everything from bugs to sex, specifically why I wouldn't have sex in the midst of so many bugs.

"Our relationship has come a long way since then," he said.

But had my tolerance for camping?

The PCT itself has come a long way since it was first conceived in the 1920s, pieces of it explored and built by youth organizations and hiking and mountaineering clubs, routes sketched and mapped by the Forest Service and other government bodies, until Congress passed the National Trails System Act in 1968. The Appalachian Trail and the PCT were the first two of the National Scenic Trails. The third, the Continental Divide Trail, is still being carved out. It took years of routing, construction, and negotiating with private property owners before the PCT was dedicated in 1993.

We took our first steps north, toward the steep slopes of California's Laguna Mountains far off in the distance. We passed a scrub oak and headed downhill into high brush. Soon we were in a low chaparral of tiny white-flowered chamise, gray-green sagebrush, and tall yuccas. The flaming red sun went down behind the dome of Hauser Mountain. Rock formations shone orange.

We wound up and down around boulders, past ribbonwood trees with their feathery bark. I forgot to be anxious and flowed with the light across the landscape. The trail undulated gently through higher brush, and just when we thought we'd lost it, it reappeared.

At 8:00 PM, we ducked behind a sandy mound to camp. Porter pulled our supper bag from his backpack, spread out the ingredients and seasonings, and set up our little stove. I fetched whatever he asked for, including his hat and jacket, but otherwise stood by at a loss.

I stared at my pack. I wanted to dig out the long underwear I would sleep in, but there was no place to unpack on. "I have to dump everything in the dirt?" I asked. Only two hours on the trail and all my stuff was dusty, with no washing machine in sight. No place to take a shower. The water we carried had to be saved for drinking.

Then Porter poured too much alcohol into our stove. Alcohol flames are invisible, so it was hard to tell whether they were burning or not. The flames leapt up and set him on fire. I screamed. He rolled over and over in the sand. Where the hell was our water? By the time I found it, he was sitting up, flames out, surveying the damage. He'd seared a big hole in his pants.

"Damn," he said.

I tried to calm down from seeing him in flames, while the evening cooled and grew quiet, pungent with sage. The desert glowed sandy pink, paled to the soft gray of the granite boulders. Darkness fell around us as we ate chili and rice from the pot Porter had cooked it in. We passed it back and forth, dug in with our plastic camping spoons. We rinsed the pot with a little of our precious water. Yucky as it was, we were thirsty, so we drank it.

Porter disassembled his homemade tin stove and repacked the food. I spread out our sleeping quilt, lined it with our foam pads, made pillows out of our jackets stuffed inside our warm hats. Too tired to put up our tarp, we crawled into our bag and fell asleep.

In the middle of the night, we were awakened by loud rock music.

"What the heck?" I whispered.

"Illegal immigrants," Porter said. "They use the trail under cover of darkness."

"Why the boombox?"

"To keep themselves company? Ward off snakes?"

We were hiking for fun, at least in theory. But ill equipped in gear, clothes, food, and water, they risked the Border Patrol, unscrupulous smugglers, imprisonment, and deportation. We'd passed a sign in Spanish, "*Cuidado! No exponga su vida a los elementos.*" Translated "Be careful! Don't expose your life to the elements," it featured pictures of a blazing sun, a coiled snake.

It seemed I'd no sooner dozed off again when I was awakened by yakking birds. "Knock it off," I yelled, and went back to sleep.

They yakked me awake again, so I lay on my back and watched the stars sink into the softening sky. I should get up. Wouldn't Porter be surprised. But I savored each minute next to him. I rolled toward him and snuggled in for as long as I could get away with it. I wanted to get to Canada; I even wanted to hike there, just not today.

When he wiggled out, I covered my head so as not to get whacked by his elbow or knee. I crawled out soon after. I picked up the two tiny antiseptic wipes I'd allotted myself for my morning ablutions and went off into the chaparral. Far from the trail, I dug my cathole, squatted, and hoped not to get bitten on the butt by a snake.

As refreshed and dainty as I was likely to get, I got lost on my way back to our campsite. I freaked, until I heard Porter's voice across the desert.

"Sweetheart, come and get it."

He'd made us hot mocha. We passed our little pot back and forth, and munched on our cereal bars. I dispensed our vitamins, my hormones and antidepressant.

"Bless Cathy's heart," I said. "If it weren't for her, I wouldn't have known I was depressed."

One visitation night, after ten years of feeling squeezed out of the family Porter had in his ex-wife and son, I broke the single most important rule of step-parenting: never disparage the kid's mother. She had called me that night about everything from Philip being allergic to strawberries to her suing us for even more astronomical child support. "What a bitch," I said to Porter when he and Philip got home from their car-chase movie. Fourteen-year-old Philip overheard; Cathy, Porter, and I duked it out at Philip's therapist's, the therapist decided that I was angry and depressed, and before I knew it, I was on a selective serotonin reuptake inhibitor.

"I feel a warm, happy glow now for Cathy," I said. Years of learning to cooperate had made us friends. "Instead of self-medicating with martinis like I was raised to by a respectable line of clinical depressives, here I am hiking the PCT on HRT and an SSRI."

We stared across the vast expanse. It was just us out here for miles. One of my reasons for hiking the trail was to finally have Porter to myself, but another emerging one was to let go of all my old issues once and for all—not just about the struggles of our marriage but all the way back through my checkered past to my own family-of-origin.

While Porter cleaned the pot and packed up the breakfast food, I stuffed our sleeping bag, Blueberry, into her waterproof nylon sack. Everything had to be packed in a certain order, Blueberry into Porter's pack first, because heavier things than our sleeping bag went on top where the weight carried better. I rolled my foam pads into cylinders to give shape to the inside of my pack, lined them with my two waterproof stuff-sacks, and filled them with my clothes and my share of the community gear, food, and remaining water.

We set off, our first full day on the trail. We hiked on dirt that was sometimes hard-packed and rocky, sometimes slippery as beach sand.

"Why do we zigzag up, down, and around each mountain?" I asked. "We're going in circles, like Dante's Hell."

"They're called switchbacks," Porter said. "Otherwise the climb is too steep."

Whatever. It took forever, and got old fast. We struggled up and around switchback after switchback, only to find—another switchback. Who knew the desert could be mountainous, instead of low and flat? At least the bushy sage and manzanita allowed for wide, shimmering vistas, dotted with purple thistle, Indian paintbrush, bluebonnets, and pink-blossomed beaver-tail cacti. That part was really fabulous.

We searched for a bit of shadow cast by a shrub, but couldn't get out of the blistering sun. Sweat evaporated from our bodies in the dry heat; our faces grew grainy with salt.

The PCT was maintained by the Pacific Crest Trail Association and other organizations. But it was still subject to detours and relocations because of wildfires, mudslides, and climate change.

Porter frowned from time to time at the map. We carried pages torn from the definitive guidebook, *The Pacific Crest Trail, Volume 1: California,* by Jeffrey P. Shaffer, Thomas Winnett, Ben Schifrin, and Ruby Jenkins.

I gazed out to the middle of nowhere. "We're lost, aren't we."

"We're not *lost*," Porter said. "We just don't know where we are."

We walked for miles. I was more than lost. What with Porter setting himself on fire, the illegal immigrants, and just plain thirst and exhaustion, I was suddenly overwhelmed with regret. I could never go home to the house we sold, painted blue with red and gold trim like a cottage in a Russian folk tale. I missed everything about it—our walls and walls of books, candlelit bedroom, and sunroom where light streamed in between the white star-jasmine. Why had we exiled ourselves from our garden of blue morning glories, red roses and hummingbird bushes, lilacs and orange trumpet vines?

Heat shimmered up in sheets from the sand. I wavered in loss, walked from mirage to mirage.

Finally Porter stopped to actually study the map. I threw off my pack and sat on it. Next thing I knew, my pack had deflated beneath me and I was in a puddle of water.

"Stand up," Porter said. "You burst your bladder."

I'd blown the stopper off the big soft-sided bottle of water I'd lugged for the last ten miles. Water we needed for drinking now soaked the inside of my pack. We'd have to make do on the water Porter carried.

We struggled down into what might be Hauser Canyon, then up the granite shoulder of what might be Morena Butte. Because I sat on our water, we had to hike hours past sunset to make it to a campground at Lake Morena. The night was pitch black, and we were so exhausted and dehydrated, we hiked two miles past our destination.

We wandered out to a remote country road, where we begged a ride back to the campground from two teenaged boys drunk on a porch. They loaded our gear into their jalopy, but slammed the trunk and sheared off the bottom six inches of my fine $220 carbon-fiber trekking poles.

"Crap," I said to Porter after they dropped us off and drove away. "What will I do without my poles?" I felt cut off at the ankles.

It was too dark to find the tent sites, so we spread out our quilt at an RV hookup. We couldn't put up our tarp because the dirt was too hard for the stakes. It's a good thing my mother isn't here to see this, I thought as I tried to fall asleep.

MY MOTHER POSTPONES DYING

I TOSSED AND TURNED FOR HOURS THAT NIGHT, my mother on my mind. Hiking the Pacific Crest Trail was an adventure she considered dangerous, even crazy. I had tried since childhood not to give her any more problems than she already had with my father's alcoholic rages and raising my two younger brothers and me. Then, in my junior year of college, I massively betrayed her. I metaphorically burned my half of our mother-daughter outfits, wore miniskirts and platform shoes instead. "You flaunt sex," she said. I had sex, and she knew it. Not the married, procreational love I'd been promised for my virtue, but the bewildering sex of the '60s, fueled by recreational drugs and loneliness.

My mother stopped speaking to me, beyond a forced cordiality, through my twenties and early thirties. I don't blame her—I was a disaster, doing the wrong things with the wrong people. I imagined I was throwing myself into the fun I didn't have the time or inclination for as a too-serious, too-responsible child. Actually, I was miserable. Was that what my mother was reacting to? I continued on the grownup track of advanced degrees, jobs, and promotions, but I seemed incapable of having a serious relationship. I found men who, like me, were afraid of real love.

In spite of her sacrifices, her efforts to be both mother and father, she hadn't been able to save me. In the end, I would have to save myself. I took myself apart, in ways my mother thought, and I refused to admit, were self-destructive, and over several years put a new self together.

Finally, I met Porter. Now I sensed that hiking the trail with him would take me apart in a different way. I went to visit my mother in Boston to tell her about our upcoming trip, and reassure her that we'd be fine. At the same time, I dreaded upsetting the fragile equilibrium we had come to since I'd married, a kind of emotionless love. We lacked the usual expressions of either endearment or conflict. I knew women who loved or hated their mothers, but none who felt the curious absence of feeling I did. Was I mirroring my mother's detachment, or was it purely my own?

I arrived at her apartment at nightfall. Outside, an ambulance siren screamed up the driveway, red and white lights flashed against my mother's windows. It was an apartment complex for older people, and someone was always being rushed to the hospital.

My mother nestled into her living room sofa in her pink robe. Nearly eighty, she looked softer, paler, and frail. She wasn't one for chitchat, so I got right to the reason for my visit.

"Mum," I said. "I have something to tell you."

She sipped at her martini. "You're getting a divorce."

"No." I wanted to laugh, but I couldn't. How could she still not believe, after seventeen years, that my marriage was happy?

Following years of relationships that had gone from bad to worse, I met Porter at a Buddhist dinner party in Houston. He had been served with divorce papers in his hospice team meeting, and Rodney, the hospice's social worker, had brought along a disconsolate Porter for the casual evening. I pulled up in my car and got out just as Porter and Rodney were unfolding their six-foot-two-inch frames from Rodney's Subaru. They looked like archangels, tall with heads of curly hair—Rodney's blond and Porter's so dark it seemed black. It was a small gathering of six, all of us neo-Buddhists. We ate, drank, and were more than a little merry, while he spent most of that evening on the phone ministering to a patient with a brain tumor, a gun, and a freaked-out wife. I was fascinated. I figured if he could cope with that, he could probably cope with me.

We married a year and a half later. The hospice chaplain who was to marry us gave us a compatibility test that proved we were irremediably incompatible. "I refuse to perform your ceremony," he said. "You're each off the charts in perfectionism, you'll have power struggles over everything." The chaplain backed out.

Undeterred, we agreed to have Porter's minister—from the Baptist church he and his ex-wife had belonged to—marry us as long as we had Buddhist buzzwords in our ceremony. The Baptist minister publicly botched the wording of our vows from "let us mindfulness pursue" to "let us mindlessness pursue."

My mother sank deeper into her sofa.

"Actually," I said, "we plan to hike the Pacific Crest Trail. From Mexico to Canada. For six months."

I sipped at my white wine while she sat there, as silent as a nondirective psychotherapist. Her silence made me uncomfortable, but I had learned not to blather compulsively to fill the void. I fought not to fall into it, not to project her possible responses, anything from "That's nice, dear," to "I think you're being foolish."

Several minutes passed. Finally she spoke.

"Well, dear," she said, "I have something to tell you. My breast cancer has returned."

I put down my glass.

"I'll come stay here, with you," I said when I found my voice, "while Porter hikes the trail." Just as I knew that she loved me and my brothers by taking care of us when our father abandoned us, I could show her I loved her by taking care of her now.

"No," she said.

No? Just "No"? She'd always been an extremely private person who savored her solitude. But not to want me there, when I might help?

I argued with myself. I would carry a satellite phone so she could reach me in the wilderness. I'd call her from each town we hiked out to for resupplies. The younger brother I helped raise lived near her, and they were comfortable with each other in a way she and I had lost. Still, it would take days to hike out to a trailhead and get to an airport.

She settled more deeply into her robe. She vacated the emotional premises. The conversation was closed.

After a sleepless night, I went out at dawn to walk on a nature path behind my mother's apartment. I began to cry, not only because she might be dying, but because the silence between us had plunged even deeper.

Porter awakened beside me in the blue dawn. People pointed at us from the windows of their RVs. We crawled out of our sleeping bag to make breakfast.

After we ate, he repaired my amputated trekking poles with string and epoxy, while I stood helplessly at the picnic table trying to understand, not to mention organize, our food. I hadn't yet accepted that we were going to be filthy for the next six months, so I washed our clothes in the water fountain and hung them to dry on the ant-covered logs that defined our site. While I was occupied, a raven pecked a hole in our food bag and gorged on our hot chocolate packets.

We got the heck out of there. The April night had been cold, but by nine, the day began to broil, eighty-five, ninety, one hundred. The Southern California sun beat down on us relentlessly and reflected up from the dry sand.

"Feel the sun-baked trail on our soles," Porter exulted, as we trudged up dusty switchbacks through cacti and yucca.

"Souls?" I asked. Mine already burned with doubt.

Later that day we sought water at another campground, but were run off by a crabby caretaker.

"We're closed," she screamed, "on account of the endangered status of the arroyo toad."

"Don't have a cow," I hollered back.

Horned toads skittered ahead of us. We tried not to step on huge furry red bugs and other horrible insects. Porter went first to watch for snakes. The trail led us between tall trees in Cottonwood Valley, then under Interstate 8 towards the Laguna Mountains. Scarlet torches of ocotillo bloomed beside barrel cactus, round and squat.

We settled into a rhythm over the next six days; we rose at dawn, ate breakfast and packed up, climbed switchbacks, stopped to rest and eat lunch. We hiked through a corner of the Anza-Borrego Desert, then across the floor of the San Felipe Valley, awash in green and yellow desert flowers. We walked through rocky ravines, uphill through thickets of white flowering chamise. I liked the calming effect of the wide landscape on my noisy mind. It felt good to just walk, put one foot in front of the other, outside in the sun and air.

But the small creek beds we passed had dried up. Parched, we came to a crossing near California Highway 78 where volunteers had left a water cache for hikers—plastic gallons roped together to keep the empties from blowing away in the desert wind. If it weren't for various kinds of volunteers, known as "trail angels," no one would survive the PCT.

We stopped to refill our bottles and eat our lunch of nuts and jerky. The air turned suddenly cold. We set off again up the mountain, in and out of canyons and gullies.

That was when we were smacked by the late-winter, early-spring storm high in the San Felipe Hills. Sleet sprang like frozen tulips from the ground, into our blowing raincoats. We both got drenched and chilled. Over the next bone-freezing hours, I struggled to remind myself I wanted to be here with Porter. But how much danger could I take? We could die of hypothermia on just our seventh day out here.

That morning Porter had written in his journal:

April 16/San Felipe Hills

I'm hoping on the trail to move past fear, unconscious patterns, materialism, and attachment. So glad to be here.

I just hoped we would survive—my mother, Porter, and I.

STREET-SMART VS. WILDERNESS-WISE

FROM MEXICO: 102 MILES. TO CANADA: 2,561 MILES.

The morning after the storm, we emerged from our sleeping bag's damp cocoon. I blinked at the sun shining on our camp at Barrel Spring.

Porter pulled stakes from the mud and ripped down our tarp. "I can't believe I almost got us killed."

Before we started the hike, I suspected I would so slow him down, he would give up. Or at the very least, he'd stay by me in the hospital in case I came out of my coma after tumbling headlong off a cliff. It never occurred to me I'd have to cheer *him* up after a narrow escape.

"You saved our lives. We would have died of hypothermia if you hadn't gotten us down the mountain and set up the tarp in record time."

He yanked on his soggy clothes. "I should have brought us more layers. Wool long johns. Rain pants."

More clothes meant more weight to carry. Would Ray Jardine, the ultralight gearhead, have brought more clothes? I wondered, WWJD: What would Jenny do? Jenny Jardine was Ray's good-humored backpacking wife.

"This is the desert," I said. "It was a freak storm. Bad weather isn't your fault."

"I'll never forgive myself if something happens to you."

Before I met him, I'd taken care of myself for so long that I was glad to find someone to share the job. I'd been responsible for myself and two younger brothers as a little girl. I grew up as street-smart as he is wilderness-wise. His relationship with the wilderness began as a coping strategy, when he went on multiday hikes to escape a boys-camp trio of bullies who physically tortured their cabin-mates. While he was a teenager learning wilderness skills at the National Outdoor Leadership School, I hid from gangs in the housing project my mother had moved us to, to get away from my father. While Porter was in medical school at Stanford, I lived in an apartment on the seedy end of Chicago's Old Town. By night I managed an R&B band; by day, I stepped over passed-out musicians on my way to my first job out of college. He became a hospice doctor and I became a librarian to prisoners and juvenile offenders. For fun, he scaled Rainier and Kilimanjaro, went rock climbing, white-water rafting, and canoeing, and led ski expeditions on Colorado's Tenth Mountain Trail, while I stayed out late at jazz clubs carousing with my friends.

"And what would I tell your mother?" he asked. "She still hasn't forgiven me for making you sleep in a culvert on our bike trip to San Diego."

That one night was a rare exception to our making it to a budget motel. It was the only shelter on a two-hundred-mile stretch of highway lined with barbed-wire fencing.

"It was a very nice culvert," I said.

I did have an adventurous side. In Houston, I ran with a group of wild Texas girls who called ourselves the Bad Girls Board of Directors, but we weren't so much bad as joyously loud, given to hilarious nights on the town. Maître d's seated us in wine cellars and party rooms so as not to disturb their more sedate patrons. We shrieked with abandon over everything from gala committee gossip to the vicissitudes of our sex lives.

My wild self balanced out my bookish, workaholic self, just as outdoor adventure balanced out Porter as a hospice doctor. What was it to be wilderness-wise, and was it a kind of wisdom I could aspire to? Three master's degrees and careers—in library science, philosophy, and writing—hadn't made me wise. What did the outdoors and "nature" have to offer me?

We packed up. He set out, me in hot pursuit, steam rising from my wet socks and shoes.

"I wanted to show you how great the wilderness is, instead of risking your life," he said. "I want you to have a good time."

"I *am* having a good time. But why do we have to hike so fast?" He was always striding, and I was always trying to catch up. Glad as I was to be with him, I was already tired of being hurried.

"That storm was nothing compared to those we'll be caught in if we don't get to Canada by mid-September. We'll have rain in Oregon and snow in Washington. But damned if I'll let us be snowbound in the North Cascades, freezing our asses off and running out of food and fuel."

We hiked past a cattle gate, then across dry Buena Vista Creek. The storm had washed the air clean of dust, but the day was heating up. The sun beamed hot yellow in the sky. The sand was dotted with cacti turning bright chartreuse.

North of San Ysidro Creek, we came to a crossing where jeep tracks nearly obscured the trail. I followed Porter northward, up-canyon, past a white-barked sycamore. We reached the canyon's rim and looked west across a valley. It was midday and we had come nine miles since breakfast. We trudged through low chaparral and dropped into grasslands and shady canyons of live oaks and cottonwoods. Pink wild roses lined the southern banks of a small stream in the valley of Canada Verde, Spanish for Green Ravine. We left the trail to walk a mile along Southern California's Highway 79 toward our first resupply stop.

Warner Springs is a tiny resort community, named for its hot spring on the Aguanga Fault. In the foothills of Palomar Mountain, it was established in 1844 as Warner's Ranch, a stop for weary travelers on the Butterfield Overland Stage. I didn't mind sleeping outside, but looked forward to a night in one of the casitas. Not to mention a hot shower and restaurant food.

But first I called my mother. I checked our satellite phone each evening for a message from her, but there never was one. To save the battery for an emergency, we didn't call out on the satellite.

"How are you, Mum?" I asked, from the pay phone at the gas station.

"Fine, dear," she said. "Your brother and I are playing Scrabble."

I pictured them at her dining room table with its flower centerpiece, the game board and their words spread out before them. "How is, what about—" I stammered, about her cancer treatment.

"Where are you?" she interrupted. That was all she wanted to know, to locate the spot on her map of the Pacific Crest Trail.

"In Warner Springs, California, one hundred and ten miles from the border of Mexico."

"Have fun," she said before she hung up. "I've got to go, your brother is winning."

Wordlessly, I handed the phone to Porter.

He called his parents, ensconced in their trilevel condo in Dallas. First he talked to his father, a man of few words, and then listened to his mother, a woman of many. His parents thought we were crazy to undertake such a hike. Porter's father particularly disapproved; at eighty, he was still going to the office. In his view, real men didn't take off six months from work. "I'll call you in the middle of the night when your mother is pacing the floor," his father told him before we left.

Porter's mother was embarrassed to tell her friends. "I'd never've sent you to camp if I'd known you'd be campin' in your fifties," she said now on the phone.

Porter stared at the phone after she hung up. "Did we do a bad thing, to take off six months from our responsibilities?" he asked me.

We'd internalized the cultural disapproval that came with our Puritan work ethic. I'd been working since I was ten. In addition to twelve-hour days at his medical practice, Porter had worked weekends writing books and articles, and doing research and expert witness work for law firms.

"We've worked our butts off," I said. "We've earned our hike."

Our hike was work of a different order. After calling our parents, we were consumed with chores. At the post office, we picked up our box of shipped food as well as the "bounce bucket" we mailed to ourselves from town to town up the trail.

"That's ours," I said of the five-gallon lidded bucket, taped with stripes of neon yellow to distinguish it from the other hikers' buckets. It was crammed with patch kits and scissors for Porter to repair our clothes and gear, blister pads and alcohol wipes, sunscreen, extra hats and gloves, long underwear, socks, even shoes.

We lugged it all back to our room. We sifted through the bounce bucket stuff and changed out gear based on what was working, what wasn't, and our best guess of the conditions that lay ahead.

Our food box—a large cardboard carton—was filled with the food we'd prepackaged at home in plastic bags for enough breakfasts, lunches, dinners, and snacks to last a week or more to our next resupply town. We dumped it all on the bed—granola bars, hot chocolate, and coffee. Peanut butter and cocktail rye, nuts and dried fruit, Snickers, Milky Ways, Toblerone chocolate. Pasta, rice, instant mashed potatoes. Dehydrated beans and tomatoes, peas, green peppers. Tuna packets, jerky. Dried sauces and seasonings.

"We have way too much food to carry, never mind eat," I said. How would we climb out of this valley with forty pounds of food, plus water?

"We'll eat it all," he said.

To hike all day, each of us needed from 6,000 to 8,000 calories—four times what we needed at home—a balance of carbs, fats, and proteins. I repacked our breakfast food in the blue stuff-sack, while Porter packed lunch food and snacks in the green and dinner in the red.

Our food finally organized, I set off to do our laundry in a beat-up washing machine with only cold water. The dirty clothes turned the water the color of coffee. I stared into it, remembered how just a few nights before we'd slept in a charred forest, on a floor of ashes, where the massive Pines Fire of 2002 had scorched thousands of acres from the Lagunas to Barrel Spring. In that ash I lost one of a pair of turquoise heart-shaped earrings I chose for the hike. Having given one to the forest, I moved the other from ear to ear every few days to keep the piercings open.

That night in the ashes, Porter wrote in his journal:

April 14/Fifty-two miles from Mexican border

Gail lost a turquoise earring. Cool wind. After stark, charred forest, magnificent vistas of the Lagunitas. Gail steady, with lots of energy, but my right blister led to Thoughts of Death. Dinner Rice-a-Roni with turkey.

While I did our laundry, Porter applied himself to making me waterproof pants—chaps like cowboys wear, but out of white trash bags—in case we ran into another storm.

"Chaps are so yesterday," I said when I saw them.

"Getting soaked in a storm is so yesterday," he said.

"Yesterday is so yesterday." It was hard to believe we started hiking the trail a little over a week ago.

The next morning, I studied Porter over our pancakes and eggs. "I don't understand your marriage," one of my friends said before we left home. I wasn't sure what she meant, beyond my puzzling willingness to follow Porter on the PCT. Did anyone understand the complex give-and-take of someone else's marriage? Ours was founded, in part, on relief at being delivered from our previous painful relationships. It evolved into a deep desire to take care of each other. As first-born children who grew to be driven adults, we understood each other's perfectionism and high expectations for ourselves. We were compatible in so many ways, it was hard to face the disparity in our physical abilities to hike the trail. Not to mention the disparity in our reasons for hiking it.

Would Porter succeed in his quest to find out who he was, beyond a hospice doctor and father to a now-grown son? Would my Good-Girl self, never good enough, and my Bad-Girl self, never bad enough to have the fun my Good-Girl missed, make peace in the space and adventure of the trail?

Was everyone out here on a quest, and how did other couples go through theirs together? Were there any other couples?

Through the café window, I saw a man and a woman wearily drop their packs. I ran out to meet them, for the first of what Porter came to call my "chatting emergencies."

"Hiking the PCT?" I asked. "Come join us for breakfast."

They staggered in and collapsed into chairs. They wore safari outfits—matching khaki hats, multipocketed shirts and pants. The man was tall and gaunt and reminded me of Abraham Lincoln. The woman was round and motherly, the kind of soft that made me want to hug her for the comfort.

"We're Tom and Sheila Pearson, from Santa Rosa, California," Sheila said.

"How far you going?" Porter asked.

"Canada," Tom said. "You?"

This was the trail call-and-response, distinguishing thru-hikers who planned to go all the way from section-hikers out for a day or a week.

"Us too," Porter said. "When did you start?" Afraid of being too old and too slow, he wanted to know how fast we were going compared to everyone else.

"Easter Sunday," Tom said.

They had started the morning after us, two weeks ahead of the pack for the same reasons we had.

"How old are you?" I asked. At fifty-six, four years older than Porter, I was the one slowing him down.

Tom was fifty-six too, Sheila forty. Neither of them had done anything like this hike before. Tom was a retired engineer; Sheila was a bookkeeper with a passion for video games. We were amazed they survived the storm in the San Felipe Hills, camped high on the mountain.

"Where'd you put up your tent in the wind and rain?" I asked.

"At least we had a tent." Tom shook his head. "Illegals wearing plastic trash bags passed us in the middle of the night."

"Yeah," Sheila said. "We just heard they were arrested here in Warner Springs."

We fell silent. We all knew what it took for the immigrants to get this far. I'd never be able to refer to illegals as "aliens" again.

Finally Tom spoke. "There's such a thing as going too light," he said. "How much do your packs weigh?"

"Eleven pounds plus food and water," Porter said.

Their packs weighed at least twice that. We marveled at their ability to go heavy, but kept quiet about what they found necessary: not just a bigger tent but a mallet to pound down tent stakes, a GPS in its own case, and God knew what else. "It'd be a serious breach of trail etiquette to criticize anyone's gear," Porter had warned me.

Tom and Porter compared gear, while Sheila and I brought each other up to speed on our families, old boyfriends, and hygiene and sex on the trail.

"It's not like we're packing sheets we can wash," I said. "Can you imagine how funky our groundcloth will be after a few times?"

That gave Sheila pause.

"I'm hiking the PCT so I can tell Porter this stuff I've told you in the last five minutes," I said.

"I'm hiking to lose fifty pounds," she said.

"We have so much in common," I said. "I'd like to lose five."

Three younger hikers joined our table—a carpenter named Karl, a pale guy named Steve, and Leather Feet, toting the hugest pack of any of us. Leather Feet was the first hiker we'd met since Peanut to have a trail-name.

We were all instant friends, with thru-hiker esprit de corps. In the wilderness, hikers were a nomadic tribe, moving roughly at the same pace but so spread out we hardly saw one another. In town, we piled up like a logjam, eating and laughing, sharing war stories and fear about the trail ahead. I looked forward to more girl-talk with Sheila.

Back in our room, Porter and I raced to finish organizing ourselves and our gear to check out by noon. While Porter sat outside at a picnic table finishing my chaps, I studied pages torn from Leslie Croot's *Pacific Crest Trail Town Guide* to figure out where to mail ahead our bounce bucket.

"Big Bear City has a post office," I said. "About one hundred sixty-five miles from here."

We hiked out at 4:00 PM, weighed down with our packs full of food. We camped above Agua Caliente Creek and purified the creek's water, as brown as our laundry's was. We dug out our heaviest dinner and ate a one-pot feast of tuna, ramen noodles, and asparagus. It felt good to be back on the trail.

In our sleeping bag, we lay on our backs on the rotating earth, and watched the moon slide across the deepening darkness. Stars punctured the night sky.

ADDICTED TO IBUPROFEN

FROM MEXICO: 120 MILES. TO CANADA: 2,543 MILES.
The next morning, we left behind the scant shade of sycamores and willows that grew near Agua Caliente Creek. All day we hiked up, down, and around switchback after switchback. We followed a sandy path through chaparral—from the Spanish word *chaparro*. These shrubs absorbed water in the winter, and fell dormant to survive the long, dry summer. At a distance, they looked the same gray-green, but up close, they were amazingly varied—white-flowered chamise, mountain mahogany, lavender yerba santa, holly-leaf cherry, sumac, sagebrush, and mountain spray. The small, stiff leaves of chaparral plants didn't wilt in the heat. Their waxy, hairy surfaces reduced evaporative water loss, and their long roots reached deep into rocky subsoil for what water there was. ·

We, on the other hand, carried our water and kept moving to find more. The dust we kicked up stuck to the sunscreen on our faces. Our khaki pants flapped at our legs, our long-sleeved shirts mopped sweat. We clutched our trekking poles with hands covered with white gardening gloves. Our wide-brimmed hats barely shaded our sunglassed eyes. These outfits made for hot walking, but we needed all this protection from the sun.

My body, aching from over a week of hiking twenty-plus miles a day, felt foreign to me on so natural a landscape. I'd been dipping into our stash of ibuprofen like a mouse into trail-mix.

Porter ached too. "It's a job climbing these hills with forty pounds of food and water, plus eleven pounds of gear."

I was carrying my own eleven pounds, and our breakfast food and tarp. And our heavy satellite phone, for lack of cell phone access, to call 911 or whatever they had out here.

In regular life, we played out the imbalances in our marriage. He worked long hours and made more money. I worked as a writer at home, and shopped, cooked, and cleaned to love on him and our house. He could fix anything; I orchestrated our social life. We complemented each other, but here the stakes were higher.

"I'm doing the best I can," I said.

But my outdoor skills left everything to be desired. I was twice as old and infinitely less experienced than most of the other thru-hikers, including the few women. Many of those hiking the 2,663-mile Pacific Crest Trail had already hiked the 2,168-mile Appalachian Trail, where I lasted only forty miles.

"I know, sweetheart," he said. "I'm just a little tired."

"Well, duh. We're walking twenty miles a day over mountains in this flaming heat with bugs, lizards, and snakes, sleeping outside to the howling of coyotes, and getting up when it's colder than a witch's tits."

"Do you want to go home?" He sounded hopeful.

"No." In a weird way, the hike was worth it.

The day didn't begin to cool until the sun started its slide down the sky about 6:00 PM. The long, late afternoon, with its radiantly gold desert light, was my favorite time to hike. I brightened at the prospect of stopping for the night, when we'd eventually get to sleep.

The evening sky softened our tension. I looked for a place to camp. His survival skills—following the route, finding water—kept us going all day, but my nesting skills helped us survive the night. I contributed that, at least, to the expedition.

"Don't worry, we'll find something," I reassured him as we rounded still one more unpromising switchback.

On the steep terrain, I searched for a campsite flat enough to spread our sleeping bag, out of the wind, on sandy rather than rocky ground. Finally I found a barely level spot far off the trail, in white sage and deer brush.

Porter found what he called a cooking rock to lean his back against while he cooked dinner. His legs stretched in front of him, he surrounded himself with the supper bag and all his spices. At home I did the cooking, but I had been reluctant to touch our alcohol stove since our first night on the trail. If Porter caught fire lighting it, I'd probably start a blaze that would scorch the desert for miles. In any case, his meals were one-pot triumphs—casseroles with noodles, cheese, vegetables, garlic, and sun-dried tomatoes.

While he cooked, I set up our wilderness bedroom.

"What do you think you're doing?" he asked, when I plugged holes in the ground with stones.

"Keeping what's down there from coming up under our sleeping bag," I said.

"Mountain lions and bears?" he asked.

"Snakes. Mice. Lizards. Scorpions. Why don't we have a tent, like Tom and Sheila?"

"It weighs a lot more, and our tarp lets in the breeze," he said.

"And the cold."

"Moisture would condense inside a tent and drip on us and our gear."

"But animals and bugs can get in a tarp," I said.

"Once trapped in a tent, they can't get out."

Which was better, a panicked mouse in our sleeping bag, or being run across all night by creatures coming and going? Resolutely, I spread out our double sleeping bag and fit the corners of our foam pads into our groundcloth's pockets.

It grew cold as soon as the sun went down, and we huddled together in our down jackets to eat the tamale pie Porter cooked. The pot warmed the hands of the one eating from it, while the other waited patiently, spork (a plastic combination of spoon and fork) in hand. Our sporks were red and orange, respectively, and bright lest we lose them in the dirt and eat henceforth with sticks.

I struggled with myself to stay out of the sleeping bag until all the chores were done—the pot cleaned, the food put away in the stuff-sacks. There was no tree from which to hang food, and we wouldn't lug our bear canister until the High Sierra. We double-bagged our food in trash-compactor bags to sleep with it under our heads. Anything that went after it would have to fight for it. Don't do this in bear country, kids.

Finally, after a couple of yoga stretches for our aching legs, we took turns wriggling into the sleeping bag. I scanned the inside with my tiny flashlight for one last bug and snake check.

In the morning, we put the stones and brush I moved back where they belonged. We adhered to the backcountry rule of "leave no trace." I liked this feel of lightness and invisibility. Instead of creating oceans of waste, we stuffed food wrappers and toilet paper into a small plastic bag we carried. Our poop was buried deep in the dirt. Instead of a polluted carbon footprint, we barely made footprints in the sand. Even these we brushed with a fallen branch before we slipped back to the trail.

We hiked down boulder-strewn side-canyons and up past Coulter pines. I was still in hiking boot camp, training to keep up with Porter. I ran haltingly; I didn't yet trust my feet not to slip in sand or stumble on roots and rocks.

He stopped and turned at my panting. "Sweetheart, you go first for a while to set the pace."

"Really?" I slid by.

"Just keep an eye out for mountain lions and bears."

Part of me would have liked to see a mountain lion or bear—in the wild, instead of a zoo. I never liked zoos, not just because I hated to see animals caged, but because it was one place my father took my brothers and me when we were small. It was meant to be a pleasant outing, my father's attempt to bond with us, but instead we were terrified he'd get drunk and leave us somewhere. He was like a caged animal himself, trapped in family life. He'd been dead for several years now, but in his restless search for himself, was the one parent who would have approved of our hike.

We walked into a burnt, desolate forest. Nothing grew in the charred sand but a single purple flower, nothing moved but a small black lizard. The only sound was the howl of wind in the stripped trees.

After the vacationlike freedom the first week of our hike, followed by our scare in the storm, we settled into a rhythm of routines. With nothing to do but walk all day, buried feelings started to emerge. Wistfulness pervaded me, like the cool, gray light. I longed to be as clean and raw as the bare Coulter pines.

Was this happening to Porter too? I suddenly noticed he was way behind me. I took off my pack and sat on a blackened rock to wait for him.

"My right foot is killing me," he said when he caught up. It couldn't be from blisters—he was adamant that at the first sign of one, we stop, take off shoe and sock, clean the "hot spot" with an alcohol pad, and apply an adhesive bandage. At every break we aired our callus-toughened feet to keep down the moisture.

While we rested, he wrote in his journal, as if making a note in a patient's chart: "Acute onset of metatarsal pain in R foot."

I'd thought that if anyone got injured, it'd be me. But if he had a foot fracture, the trip was over. Just when I was starting to like it.

"Let's redistribute our gear," I said. "I've got to carry more of my share."

"No," he said.

"Yes."

Reluctantly, he handed over one of our food bags. I handed him a couple of our ibuprofen and water to wash it down.

He sat there gloomily.

"I'm sorry your foot hurts," I said.

"It's not just that," he said. "I thought hiking the PCT would help me regroup after leaving the hospice. But now I can't stop thinking about how I could have saved it."

"You'll find another job, in another hospice," I said. "Although hospice work seems so depressing, everyone wondered how you stood it."

"What's depressing is that our cultural fear of dying makes it worse than it should be. It's actually a meaningful part of life, especially if you're not in pain or tormented with needles and tubes."

Working with the dying had been life-giving for him, and the other doctors, nurses, nurse's aides, social workers, and chaplains who made up the hospice team. Once they got the person's symptoms under control, they and their family breathed a sigh of relief. Heck, the person sometimes lived longer, fully conscious, and certainly more comfortably. They could die in dignity and peace, often at home surrounded by family and friends.

"Our lives pass so quickly," he said after a while. "When you spend your days taking care of people who are dying, you can't help but ask, 'Who am I? What's my life for?'"

I followed his gaze toward the horizon, where low mountains met the sky. We were long past answering these questions the way we had in our twenties, or even in the midlife crises of our forties. The older we grew, the deeper the question plunged.

He stood up, shouldered his pack. We kissed, and his wet tears slid down my cheeks.

"Dying may be a meaningful part of life," I said, "but let's not do it yet." Whether headed for death or just down the trail, I was going too.

We walked on, over the fire-scarred ridges. The skeletal remains of these black oaks, white firs, incense cedars, and Jeffrey pines would have to pass through several stages of vegetation before a new forest grew.

We were silent for miles, stunned by the mountains opening around us, snowy San Gorgonio Peak and nearer, San Jacinto Peak and the rocky spine of the Desert Divide. Below sprawled the Anza and Terwilliger valleys. The Santa Rosa Mountains rose above the desert floor. Over much of Southern California, we would climb up to the windy peaks and plunge down again into the desert valleys' broiling heat.

But Porter's foot pain worsened. We plodded down to Pines-to-Palms Highway 74 and hobbled along it to the Paradise Café.

"What should we do?" I asked him over our Jose Burgers, said to be the biggest, juiciest, most loaded with trimmings near the trail.

He didn't answer. Food was one of his favorite things, but now he ate so morosely I was worried. Staring out the café window, I spotted a car about to drive off.

I tore out. "Can we catch a ride with you into Idyllwild?" I begged the young couple.

Perplexed, they answered in German.

I mustered the only German I remembered from my trip to Europe thirty years ago with three gay guys, which translated to "Excuse me, where is the youth hostel?"

They waited while I ran back into the Paradise Café, thrust our trekking poles at Porter, and grabbed our two packs. "Limp," I commanded him, and we piled with our gear into their rental car.

Michael and Sabine went out of their way to drive us fifteen miles into the resort town of Idyllwild, high in Southern California's San Jacinto Mountains, with a population under 4,000. We asked at a tiny appliance store where to find a doctor. Michael, arms heavily tattooed, insisted on giving Porter a clean shirt to wear into the doctor's office. The doctor X-rayed Porter's foot and assured him he'd recover from his inflamed metatarsal bones if he stayed off it for a few weeks. The doctor's receptionist drove us to a small inn surrounded by ponderosa pines, and the innkeeper drove into town to pick us up a pizza.

"Aren't we glad we brought that gun to protect us from all the scary people everyone said we'd run into?" I joked over our pizza.

Porter was too upset to laugh. "I can't stay off my foot for weeks."

Ensconced in the inn filled with heavy Victorian antiques, he applied himself to making waterproof mittens to attach to our raincoats, as well as a vapor barrier liner bag to keep us warm in an emergency.

Over the next few days, I walked down the cedar-scented road into town. I hiked through the narrow streets to do laundry, bought and repacked groceries for the next nine-day section to Big Bear Lake, and shipped ahead supplies.

I found Internet access at the public library and wrote a cheery email home:

Dear family and friends,

We think of you as we trek over these gorgeous mountains on a moderate grade, sometimes through broad meadows, the sandy trail bordered by wildflowers—baby-blue-eyes and purple chia, California poppies. We can't get over how kind everyone is.

Porter is an outdoor culinary genius.

We're grateful for all your love and support. We're getting what we came for, even if we don't know what that is.

I called my mother, and again didn't get much from her about her illness. Still, it was odd how much closer I felt to her from here, so far away. It was nearly Mother's Day, and I shopped for a gift for her that expressed my hope that we were each where we were meant to be. I settled on turquoise agate wind chimes, and coral agate chimes for Porter's mother. I loved to give presents because they put me in touch with how much I loved, deep down, the people I gave them to.

Back at the inn, I showed Porter the gifts.

"How's your mother doing?" he asked.

"She said she's okay. I don't know what to do but take her word for it."

"We're not going to change our parents," Porter said. "The best we can do is love them for who they are."

"Do you think your mother will like her wind chimes?"

"No," he said. "But she doesn't like anything we give her."

"What would she like?"

"For me and my two brothers to sit beside her holding her hand, telling her how much we love her every minute for the rest of her life."

I laughed, but our mothers were exact opposites of each other. My mother asked for nothing, and this too troubled me. She thanked me politely for every gift, and then put it away in a box for me, for after she died. When I was young, she used whatever I gave her, an inexpensive pair of earrings, or a small household item like an ashtray or a sugar bowl. We had so little, we needed everything. Now we had everything, and needed nothing but the love we seemed incapable of expressing.

Having run out of sewing projects by our third night in Idyllwild, Porter insisted on testing his foot by walking down the road to dinner at Café Aroma. We stuffed ourselves on manicotti smothered in tomato sauce, chicken parmigiana, and flaky chocolate-laced profiteroles. The servers burst into operatic song for the diners.

"We're outta here," Porter said after dinner, newly fortified. "Inflamed metatarsal be damned."

He was still limping the next morning when town resident Patti Lovejoy gave us a ride back to the trail. Her son, trail-named Molasses, was out hiking some other section of the PCT, she wasn't sure where.

"I feel like I'm helping him," she said, "when I help you."

We got out of the car at the trailhead.

"Happy Mother's Day, Patti." I leaned in the car window to give her a hug.

She grinned and hugged me back.

LEARNING TO WALK

FROM MEXICO: 151 MILES. TO CANADA: 2,512 MILES.

I was beginning to love the trail. It lay down before me and beckoned with branch and flower. I followed it, even when it tripped me with roots, wilted me with heat.

How would I rise to the challenges of the trail as I had those of our marriage? Our marriage was tested over and over our first seventeen years. For the first few, I was terrified that Porter was having an affair. I had left a previous long-term lover because he was unfaithful, and Porter was nothing like him. Still, I worried. Before Porter, I'd gravitated toward men with the untrustworthiness of my father, the distance of my mother. For whatever reason, I had what were called "trust issues," and it pissed the hell out of me about myself.

I had no reason to think Porter was having an affair, except that I regularly smelled perfume on his lapels. He was mystified, until he sniffed them himself. "Who was in the car with you today?" I demanded when I smelled it there. "Mary, the hospice nurse, on our home visits, as usual," he said. In her sixties, Mary was a happily married Catholic with five kids. I adored her; she and her husband, Ted, had helped us move into our house. No way were Porter and Mary having an affair. Not to mention that hospice workers, standing with grieving families around the bedsides of dying patients all day, hug each other all the time.

Porter wasn't having an affair, but his ex-wife lived a mile from us, and it seemed to me she kept their relationship alive with agitation, not just lawsuits for more child support but changes in our visitation schedule. It was the price he had to pay for time with his son. How could I argue with that? Various people advised me to have a child myself. "You need to become a family of your *own*," one said. But Porter couldn't imagine adding to the emotional turmoil in our lives. I knew he loved me enough to have a child if I really wanted, but I was ambivalent. I was afraid, as my mother was, that I wouldn't be able to protect a child in so dangerous a world. It wasn't just untrustworthy men, or poverty, or wars. My sense of danger was an inherited state of mind.

What did I do? I signed Porter and me up for dance lessons. It seemed to me that learning to dance together was one thing we could do just ourselves, apart from my past, apart from his ex-wife and his son, his long hours at the hospice, his ongoing history with his mother.

He had never liked to dance. He associated it with being forced by his mother to take girls he didn't particularly like to one debutante ball after another. All he could really do when I met him was the "hippie noodle" that passed for dancing at Stanford in the '70s. But he wanted to please me, and dancing was a lot easier than having a baby together.

The ballroom dance class was held in the gym at our local community center, under fluorescent lights. Our teachers, Mr. and Mrs. Lark, taught us the foxtrot—step, step, side, together. The foxtrot didn't come easily to Porter, and I already knew how. Nor would he let me show him, so I followed his mistakes. We shuffled in a circle around the floor, moved with the other couples in a vague direction called the "line of dance." Mr. Lark played the same Arthur Murray foxtrot music track over and over on his CD player.

Porter gave up on the steps; he just couldn't do them. His left leg was behind him in a travesty of a cross-step when I tripped over his right and collapsed across his left hip. We were laughing like naughty eighth-graders when we heard a crash. Mrs. Lark had fainted on the other side of the room. She lay on the floor in a straight line as if she had fallen like a tree, without crumpling from the knees or trying to break her fall.

Porter took charge and determined that she was still breathing.

She came to, crying softly. "I broke my tooth."

"Can you move your jaw?" Porter felt for broken bones in her wrists, her ankles.

Mr. Lark stood back helplessly. He looked grief stricken, his wife doing something he couldn't be part of. I found the piece of Mrs. Lark's tooth on the floor, picked it up and handed it to her husband. The ambulance arrived, and the rest of us went home.

The vision of Mrs. Lark face down on the floor took a deep hold on my mind. "That shouldn't have happened to her," I said to Porter. "She was so empathetic and instructive."

The rest of our classes were cancelled. It didn't matter, though. Porter had shown his love by his willingness to try dancing with me, just as I was now trying to hike with him.

The San Jacinto was the first major range of the Pacific Crest Trail with elevations above 10,000 feet. From just under 5,000 feet at Pines-to-Palms Highway, we began to climb, up through brush, along a ridge top, in and out of ravines. The constant up and down made it hard to feel progress. We'd ascended many more than 1,000 feet by the time we reached a 6,000-foot-high saddle on the Desert Divide.

The ridge of the Desert Divide ran from Toro Peak north to Red Tahquitz in the southern San Jacinto mountain range. I felt the divide in myself. On one hand, I loved the panoramas, west to evergreen mountains, east into rolling valleys, north to snowy peaks, south to desert canyons. I wanted to learn to hike like I dance. On the other hand, I was beginning to decompose like the granite beneath my feet. Maybe progress wasn't the point, but I didn't know how to stop thinking in terms of progress. I felt as if I were running backwards, my feet fighting for traction in rocky flakes of schist. After another exhausting scramble, I couldn't hold back my tears.

"I'm wiped," I said.

"Here, eat." Porter fed me nuts and chocolate, and held the water bottle to my lips.

"I'm okay."

"I'm worried about you," he said.

I was worried about him and his foot. I was worried about myself. What would get me through this? Like the canyons crumbling into the land between Red Tahquitz and San Jacinto peaks, I was eroding into the landscape of myself. Legend had it that a Cahuilla Native American demon devoured Indian maidens here, but I had no spirit to blame.

I was embarrassed to be caught crying when a hiker overtook us and stopped in concern. Wiry, he was dressed like a runner in shorts and thin shirt, a miniscule pack over one shoulder. Porter hated being passed by younger, stronger guys, and once again I felt like the little old lady slowing him down.

"Doing okay?" the man asked.

"Fine." Porter shook his hand. "We're Porter-and-Gail."

"Scott," he said.

I looked up, startled. "Scott Williamson?"

He nodded modestly. We'd heard of this legendary thru-hiker back at Warner Springs. Not only hiking the PCT north in record time, this season he would turn around at the Canadian border and thru-hike south in record time back to the border of Mexico.

"Wow," Porter said. "How many other thru-hikers have you passed?"

"About ninety since the Mexican border." He smiled.

We were ahead of not only those ninety, but also the two hundred who hadn't yet started when Scott hit the trail. It gave me a lift; it's more fun to be near the front of the pack than lagging behind at the end. By the time the stragglers got to the rare water caches, the plastic jugs were empty. The shelves of convenience stores in obscure towns were already wiped clean.

For company, you had only the lame and the halt instead of the boisterous clan.

While Porter and Scott talked in man-grunts, I breathed sighs of relief. I felt safer knowing that whatever happened to us on the trail, someone would come along to help. Even Scott, as fast as he was hiking, stopped to check on us.

"How does he do it?" I asked when he flew on up the mountain.

"He's a different species," Porter said.

We hiked on to the North Fork San Jacinto River and a waterfall icy with snowmelt. We caught the water in our cooking pot to distribute into our four one-liter bottles and the six-liter one. It would have to last us to Snow Creek at the northern base of the San Jacinto Mountains, a brutal twenty-five miles from here.

Porter was exhausted too, and collapsed to the ground at the end of the day. After catching on fire lighting the stove our first night on the trail, he'd been careful not to add too much fuel. But this time the wind seemed to have blown out the invisible flames. He poured more alcohol on the stove. Fire shot in a streaming arc to his hand. He jerked it back. Alcohol spewed from the bottle to his pants, his pack, his mat—they all caught fire. Orange-yellow flames surrounded him in the darkness.

I screamed, but had more presence of mind than I did the first time. I ran to him with the six-liter bucket of water we had lugged all day up the mountain.

"No!" he said.

I stopped in my tracks. I watched, horrified, while he beat out the flames with his hands, then dribbled a little cool water on them.

"This is insane," I shouted. "You're more freaked out about wasting water than burning to death."

He fell silent. He stared at the second-degree burns on one hand for so long I was frightened. His stoicism struck me as bizarre. Once, enraged at his resignation in the face of his ex-wife's demands, I threw my wedding ring at him. But we weren't back there early in our marriage, we were here.

"I know it hurts," I said. What was it that kept him from saying so?

"Damn," he said finally. "I feel like an idiot."

After what happened to poor Mrs. Lark, we didn't have the heart to try ballroom again. I was still fine with not having a child if we could learn some kind of dance together, so we tried disco lessons at a place called Two Left Feet.

"Studio 2," sighed our teacher, Penny, a petite androgyne with punk copper hair and a baby on her hip. With her frown and lipstick-lined pout, she looked like she'd had a hard life with many disappointments in love.

We filed with the other students into the windowless room, black except for two long walls lined with mirrors. The effect was of claustrophobia and vertigo at the same time. Porter leaned his elbows on the dance bar, which fell loudly off the wall.

Penny parked her baby on some cushions. "Always start on your right foot," she began, as seriously as if telling us how not to get pregnant.

She showed our class the basic step, side to side, then twists with each foot out front. She insisted we hold up our hands so they wouldn't flop around. "So you won't look as if you don't give a fuck," she said.

We caught glimpses of ourselves in the mirror, looking truly absurd. We were all missing some ingredient between the step and the style. Penny taught each step her way, then the way her supervisor had told her to teach it.

"Don't y'all think that looks dorky?" she said of her supervisor's way.

"You're asking us?" Porter said.

Finally we had to go through all the steps with music. Penny called out the patterns and got confused, but I didn't mind. I wanted her to keep her job and succeed in life. I watched Porter struggle valiantly through the routine, and my heart flip-flopped with love. Left to his own devices, he certainly wouldn't be there.

"It's ridiculous to call that 'freestyle' disco," he said after class as we walked to our car.

"Even freestyle has steps," I said.

"Do you mean to tell me those steps are going to look like something on the dance floor?" He fumed the way he does, wordlessly but somehow so loudly that I felt compelled to respond.

"Look at it this way," I said. "You have to put your feet somewhere."

I had to put my feet somewhere, I told myself the next morning on the trail. Porter's seared hand in a bandage, we walked along. I grounded myself in my marriage as it was now, even as I pondered our first seventeen years and wondered what lay ahead for us.

It was hard to believe it was spring in Southern California, when the lower desert broiled with heat and the high desert still had snow. The trail above 8,000 feet on north-facing Fuller Ridge was hidden by heavy snowpack. We negotiated its icy glaze. I focused on staying upright, but fell time and again. My clothes got soggy. I couldn't recover my balance. I was much more of a klutz hiking in snow than Porter was trying to dance. I wore out, struggling up painfully with my pack.

Except for a few tears, I had done so well up to then. I wasn't just physically, but emotionally unprepared for this steep, rocky terrain, the sweltering climbs up sun-baked ridges, and now this sinking and falling in snow. Fear shot through me with each fall. I sank into failure, icy, wet. I struggled up on shaking legs. Falling, failure, exhaustion. The spaces between separate falls shrank until I was falling over and over with hardly any upright in between.

"Damn it," I shouted. The woods ring with my anger: *Damn it, damn, damn.*

I was embarrassed by my ineptitude and rage. I couldn't understand the layers of my anger, its causes and displacement. Deep as the snow, how far back did it go?

What was it like for me to learn to walk after my second birthday, when my baby shoes were finally unscrewed from the brace? I couldn't remember, the memory was locked not just in my legs but my whole body and brain. I must have felt the natural imperative to walk, mixed with pride and courage and fear. My mother must have helped me, encouraged me to walk toward her. I stepped and fell, stepped and fell again.

Hiking in deep snow was like learning to walk.

"I'll go first and make footprints," Porter said now. He spaced them narrowly enough in the snow that I could match his stride.

But I couldn't match his skill. I fell hard, sideways, on a boulder.

"Shit." My shoulder seared with pain.

Porter unbuckled my pack and lifted it off. I staggered to my feet. Carefully, he felt my shoulder and all around it.

"I don't think it's broken," he said, "but you probably tore the muscle that covers your shoulder joint."

"Tore my shoulder muscle? How will I carry my pack?" Furious with myself, I sounded angry with Porter. I was angry, period, although it was neither of our faults. That infuriated me further, this tendency in myself to look for someone to blame. Shit happens. Why couldn't I give myself, and Porter, a break?

He knelt and took weight from my pack, my share of the community gear and water.

We went on, descended, then clambered around wind-beaten trees. We rounded a switchback, and I forgot my pain at the view of hulking San Gorgonio Peak. Seven thousand feet below lay San Gorgonio Pass, between branches of the San Andreas Fault. The setting sun softened the glare from the snow-flecked mountains, deepened the shadows in the green valleys.

We camped among ponderosa pines and white firs. In spite of our soft pine-needle bed, I began a pattern of painful sleep. My shoulder ached where I had torn my anterior deltoid. As soon as I lay down my legs began a deep neuromuscular twitching, like an itch I couldn't get at. They jumped as if they couldn't stop hiking. I was asking too much of them, walking more than twenty miles a day, day after twelve-hour day. Pain in my quadriceps, the extensor muscles at the front of the thigh, woke me hourly. I shifted position all night, desperate for relief, waking Porter with my tossing and turning.

"Why don't my legs and shoulder hurt while I'm hiking?" I asked him. "Why do they wait until it's time to go to sleep?"

He didn't answer, just massaged them in sympathy. Back home, I had asked him what it would be like to sleep on the trail. "You'll be tired, but it will be a good tired," he'd said.

I contemplated the Coulter pines, with cones the size of pineapples. Even in my agony, they seemed wise, benevolent presences. They swayed so slowly they appeared to be dancing in place.

I used to put on disco CDs and practice dancing during the week. I did it when Porter wasn't home, because I didn't want him to feel pressured.

"You don't have to go to dance class anymore," I told him. "It's okay with me if you never go again."

"I'm going," he said.

But Penny had been fired. Would she find another job? What about the baby?

Porter liked Dan, our new teacher, who explained dancing in terms of science and athletics. "You bend your knees because it gives you a lower sense of gravity," Dan said. "It gives you more energy, it gives you better—what?"

"Balance," our class recited in unison. In contrast to Penny's distracted chatter, Dan left out the last word in each sentence to make us participate.

"That's what we mean by getting—?" Dan asked.

"Down."

"Do you stay level?" Porter asked him.

"Let's find that out." Dan picked up a yardstick.

Leave it to a man to bring a yardstick into a dance studio.

Porter held the yardstick horizontally behind Dan's shoulders while he executed some steps. "Was I level or what?" Dan asked.

"Pretty much," Porter said.

"I don't know who made up these steps, people," Dan said. "But if you do them, you can pass. You'll notice on any dance floor, only 5 percent are really good, the other 95 are just doing what they can. It's like anything else, people, the more you do it, the better you get. My goal is just to get you out there. You've learned enough to get by."

"I'd take any dance class that guy offered," Porter said on our way home.

"Seriously? He danced in a manly way, for sure."

"He made me want to dance like him."

"He was good," I said. "And he was straight, to boot."

"I really don't care what his sexual preference is."

After that, Porter and I were up and running in the dance department. We learned disco, the cha-cha, and swing, but the bump became our specialty. We did it everywhere from wedding receptions to hospice galas, and shocked Porter's mother by doing it at a debutante ball.

PILGRIMAGE

FROM MEXICO: 200 MILES. TO CANADA: 2,463 MILES.

We pounded down and around countless switchbacks out of the San Jacinto Mountains. In just eighteen miles, we descended 7,000 feet. With the drop in altitude, we found ourselves in an entirely new ecosystem, from the deer and wildcats in the snowfields to lizards and snakes in the sagebrush. We moved through our own shifting ecosystems of body, mind, and heart.

I could almost feel the creaking and groaning of the earth in the visceral plunge and soar of the mountains. Earthquakes over eons carved the steep traverses of the north–south San Jacintos and Lagunas, the east–west San Bernardinos and San Gabriels.

We crossed the San Andreas Fault, only to face another challenge: wind. Porter's foot hurt from the extra weight he took on when I couldn't keep my balance in the snow, and now from staying upright in this knock-you-over wind.

We were used to the blowing in the mountain passes, but this was much fiercer. Strong coastal gales poured air into the hot desert of San Gorgonio Pass to make a violent wind tunnel between the San Jacinto and San Bernardino mountains.

We found our way through a steely forest of windmills, towering so high they made us shudder. They turned wind into energy, its roar into a ghostly drone.

With no place to camp out of the wind, we pushed hard into it to make it to the "Pink Motel." Finally, in a maze of junkyards, we came upon not a motel at all but two trailers, one sun-bleached pink, cobbled together in a sea of rusted metal.

An elderly couple, who at that time let hikers sleep in the trailers, came out of their house to greet us.

"You can sleep on the floor of this trailer," the man said.

"And use the kitchen in the other," the woman added.

We were relieved to be out of the wind. I heated water for pasta. It came to a boil right before the propane burned out. Porter and I were sitting down to eat when another thru-hiker tumbled in.

"I'm Pine Needle," he said.

Pine Needle? What a humble trail-name for so large and prepossessing a man. "You're just in time for dinner," I said.

"You sure?" He must have been as ravenous as we were, but stood back in a courtly way.

Porter pulled up a chair for him, and the three of us ate under a bare bulb battery-powered by wind-turbine. The roaring wind shook the trailer. I was too tired to do anything but listen while Porter and Pine Needle talked. Their conversation moved from gear to God.

"I'm hiking the trail to raise contributions for mission work in Nicaragua," Pine Needle said.

"I'm grateful to God to be out here," Porter said.

Pine Needle lifted his Bible. "I'm glad to have time to read this."

"How much does that weigh?" I asked.

They stared at me for a moment, and then went back to their God-talk.

I was once devout, like Pine Needle. At the Catholic girls high school I went to, I poured my burgeoning passions into ecstatic religiosity. Each morning, I happily pinned my starched white collar onto my navy blue uniform with tiny safety pins, and folded the white handkerchief with the school's pale blue emblem into my breast pocket. Some girls' mothers embroidered elaborate lace borders onto their pocket-handkerchiefs. My mother had enough to do, working full time at a library and raising my brothers and me. I bought lace edging at Woolworth's, and sewed it on myself.

"Sister, may I go to Chapel?" I'd ask, during study hall. I tiptoed down the long corridor to the convent, where the chapel was. The convent, like the school, was fragrant with waxed linoleum, mahogany polished to a lemony finish, the clean smell of starch.

The chapel itself smelled of incense. I sat there alone, in the middle of the school day, feeling like I was getting away with something. I felt a nameless presence, more alive than I myself.

Pine Needle stayed up to read his Bible under the bare bulb, while Porter and I headed for the other trailer to sleep. Between the kitchen trailer and the sleeping trailer, I was nearly knocked down by the wind. I'd fallen and staggered up so many times in the last couple of days that I'd reenacted my own version of the Stations of the Cross. My shoulder hurt so much I must be being punished. I was taught by the nuns to "offer up" my sufferings for Christ. "I don't believe in that offer-it-up crap," my mother once said, to her credit.

"When my shoulder hurts," I said to Porter now, as we went into the trailer, "I should think of it as picking up my cross."

"No," he said. "It means you should put your cross down."

We retreated into the stillness of the trailer, all the more silent for the wind howling outside. After all our efforts to hone down our gear, we ourselves were being honed—by wind, sand, and the sheer effort of climbing and descending hour after hour, day after day. I was being stripped bare of the trappings of an unessential self—deconstructed, unmasked.

I had tried to pare myself down to an essential self before I married Porter, spending three months in total silence in a

Buddhist monastery. Like me, everyone in the meditation hall seemed hell-bent on finding peace. Some of us swayed sleepily like bottom-heavy beanbag toys on our sitting cushions. Others sat rigidly upright, as if fighting to contain their restless bodies and minds, to not jump out of their skins. Still others sat in calm repose, at once quiet and vibrantly alive.

Is peace what we were after out here? Porter too had tried other avenues. His own interest in meditation led him to the Christian mystics and the contemplative prayer of Roman Catholics. Then, ten years into our marriage, he decided to do a private weekend retreat at a convent in Houston. I was shocked. I'd long stopped thinking of myself as a fallen-away Catholic, in favor of recovering Catholic, even born-again pagan. But he had none of the baggage—misogyny, Lenten morbidity, sexual shaming—that were as much a part of the Boston Irish Catholicism I grew up with as May processions and Holy Communion.

"I understand Catholics," I had said to Porter. "I'm coming along on this retreat to protect you."

We drove through the iron gates of the convent grounds, an oasis of greenery in a deteriorating part of the city. Sister Mary Presentation showed us to our rooms on separate floors of the dormitory. On the women's floor, she pointed past a giant alabaster statue with wings. "Just turn left at the angel," she told me. Each room had the name of a saint on the door. "You're in Mary Magdalene." That figured.

Then she left us to our own devices. In silence, we visited the Oratory with its candle glowing in the sanctuary lamp. We followed the scent of incense to the meditation room, with votive candles, a Bible open on a table, comfortable chairs, even a couple of Buddhist meditation cushions. The ambience was a strange but comforting mix of anachronistic old-world Catholicism and ecumenical new-age spirituality.

Nevertheless, we were taken aback that a massage came with our retreat fee. I went for the first one, while Porter went to receive spiritual direction from Sister Mary Presentation. The masseuse, who came in from the outside as a form of spiritual service, was young and pretty. Porter will love this, I thought.

While Porter had his massage, I wandered the convent's fenced-in grounds. It was also the nuns' cemetery, and the plain headstones were inscribed with only their names, dates they were born, entered the convent, and died. I looked up to see Porter running toward me in a panic.

"What's the matter?" I forgot we were in silence. "You're supposed to be all chilled out from your massage."

"It was awful, I couldn't relax," he said. "If I'm going to be massaged by a woman, it would help if she weren't good-looking."

I didn't have time to reply, due at my appointment for spiritual direction with Sister Mary Presentation.

"What parish do you belong to?" she asked.

"I don't, actually." I hesitated. "Actually, I don't go to church."

"Do you at least read the Scriptures?"

"I read the Bible quote on the editorial page of the newspaper," I said. "I cut it out and put it in my husband's lunch along with a cartoon."

She paled. She reminded me of my Aunt Mary, in a shawl and sensible shoes, just before she fell and broke her ankle coming out of Mass. Poor Aunt Mary. She was my godmother, and I loved her, but she'd turn over in her grave if she knew I was not just a recovering Catholic and recovering Buddhist, but a recovering everything.

"What do you believe, then?" she asked.

"I try not to think about it too much," I said. "But if I had to say, I just want to be one with my true nature." Whatever that was.

She looked at me, and I looked at her. In her eyes, I saw the recognition of a mystery neither of us could articulate, but knew, all the same.

We were up before the stars faded from the sky. Pine Needle had already left. It was hot by 6:30 AM when we began a hard hike

7,000 feet up into the San Bernardino Mountains. We left the lower Sonoran desert for the higher one of sparse chaparral and sharp cacti. The heat rose to over a hundred degrees. We turned and looked back at yesterday's snow-covered Fuller Ridge, high in the San Jacintos.

"We climbed that?" I asked.

It was so hot that by midmorning, we'd had to drink all of our water. Rounding a switchback, we came upon Pine Needle reading the New Testament. Too parched to talk, we nodded and passed by.

Porter and I gave each other a glazed stare. Deprived of water, blood thickened and decreased circulation, raising blood pressure. The muscles didn't get enough oxygen, the brain slowed down. Neither of us was thinking straight. I was too scared to cry.

We sluggishly walked on. We hadn't had to urinate in hours. I didn't need to ask Porter the signs of dehydration, I was experiencing them firsthand—queasiness, headache, aching joints.

Waves of heat rippled from the sand. Up ahead, glassy pools of water shimmered, only to be gone when we got there. In my near-hallucinatory state, I saw physical things—shrubs, rocks, and lizards—so abstractly they seemed not images but dissolving fragments of thought. I struggled to hold on to my thinking even as it floated away like the ripples off the sand.

Hours later, we found water at Whitewater Creek, which the guidebook had said might be dry from the California drought.

"Please tell me it's not a mirage," Porter said.

Water rushed over white boulders of granite and marble. I stood at the edge, wavered like a heat mirage myself. Almost in a shared hallucination, Porter and I unpacked our water-purifying drops and bottles by the creek. With a patience that belied our thirst, we filled the bottles and waited for the chemical reaction of the drops. We sank to our knees in the creek. Finally we drank our fill.

After a while, we pushed on, past red basalt rock formations and across dry sandy washes. Scrub brushed and scratched our legs. The trail was eroded by mudslides from fires in the San

Bernardinos. I'd graduated to carrying the heavier dinner bag instead of the lighter breakfast one, but I was crumpling from the weight in such heat.

Even rehydrated, I had to fight to put one foot in front of the other. "This is really hard," I said. "I hurt all over. My pack is too heavy for the pain in my shoulders."

Unable to continue climbing through the midday heat, we stopped to make lunch our main meal. We would have to hike longer into the hopefully cooler evening. Porter cooked chili with rice. Hot chili was the last thing I wanted. We passed our pot gloomily between us.

"I don't know what to do about our pack weight division," he said after a while. "If you carry even a third of the total weight, you fall apart. If I carry two-thirds or more, my right foot hurts like hell."

"I've got to get stronger," I said. But how?

"Not to mention the emotional strain," he went on. "We want to do the hike together, but you've never attempted anything this hard."

Fewer than two hundred twenty-five miles into our hike, this didn't bode well. We weren't even a tenth of the way. I hurt enough to come off the trail. Did Porter want or not want me here? I was both a comfort and a problem.

We finished our chili and walked on. Finally we stopped on a ridge top to camp for the evening in a swarm of gnats.

Should I leave the trail? Its hardships seemed a test of my worthiness. Where would I go? From our ridge top, I stared down into deepening darkness.

A few lights blinked on below. Over the next hour, they spread into a shimmering oasis.

"What can that be?" I asked Porter.

"Palm Springs," he said.

What was that doing there? A year before, we'd been in Palm Springs for a hospice physicians' meeting. We listened to live jazz while we dined on ahi tuna and sipped champagne. I loved its laid-back '50s elegance and quirky attractions—Liberace's home, and celebrity names imprinted in the sidewalks. Could I hang out there while Porter hiked the trail?

I looked down at the far-below glitter of Palm Springs, then up to the sky and the stars—alarmingly close, shocking stabs of light.

I was stunned that I wouldn't be anywhere else but here. I didn't recognize myself. I wasn't on a hike, or even a retreat, but a pilgrimage. How could I leave before it finished its work on me? Chastened by hardship, in awe of the mountains, soul-shaken by wind, I desperately wanted to go on. My discomforts were small inside the vastness of this space, to which I too belonged. I was dwarfed by everything. This mountain, like the others, was enormous. Just as the daytime sky was infinitely blue, the night was so deep.

Later that night I was awakened by a light shining in my eyes—the moon, too bright for sleep. I wanted to cry out from its closeness, on this ridge between mountain and sky. I lay on my back and gathered myself in the gusts beneath ancient trees.

SEX UNDER THE TARP

FROM MEXICO: 222 MILES. TO CANADA: 2,441 MILES.
I woke up on our small flat spot. The sun rose and pink-orange light melted over the dark green mountains. I watched Porter sleep, and marveled again at the love I felt for him the moment I met him. It wasn't a calculation or a feeling. I could barely allow myself a sexual attraction, really, suspended as sex was for me between degradation and sublimation. But something in me recognized him through my psychosexual fog.

Before I met Porter, I was in love for years with two men at the same time. One, whom I'll call R, was my boyfriend, and we had a wild ride of a love affair fraught with his infidelities and my fits of rage. He had a lot of money and wined and dined me, took me to costume balls and lavish parties where he'd abandon me as soon as we walked in so he could work the crowd. At those events, I sipped champagne and wandered through a sea of strangers, mostly older, my parents' age. I was young and beautiful and could speak intelligently on a variety of topics. No one seemed to notice that my evening gowns came from the nightgown department at Sears. Over time, R dressed me for the part, in preppy blazers and leather purses for polo games, trim white pants and Lacoste shirts to watch him compete in tennis tournaments, black lace dresses for orgies. I didn't have to do anything at his parties, just be there, an object of desire. It was a dangerous game I played with my own heart.

I confided in another man, whom I'll call E. He shook his head ruefully and worried about me, but was in no position to do anything but listen. He was married, highly moral and faithful to his wife, and our relationship remained completely platonic. He listened to me so attentively that I felt deeply understood. It wasn't until he met my eyes that I realized no one—*no one*—had ever really looked me in the eye before. I felt so safe with him that my love for him became an almost spiritual obsession, and he treated my adoration with wary affection.

R, on the other hand, was always distracted when I was with him, either flirting with another girl or plotting aloud some new investment scheme. Women and money were his obsessions. He was charming, he could dance, he had great taste. He awakened in me a love for life's pleasures, and I let him take me to resorts and exclusive clubs where I could secretly daydream of E.

R acted out his own psychosexual conflicts by trying to seduce other women in my presence. Pride kept me from throwing a fit in public, but at home I dumped out dresser drawers and tore his clothes from my closet in a tangle of twisted coat hangers. He'd moved in part-time with me, and with how many others? "You're so violent," he said, but he liked me that way. He purposely incited jealousy in me, and I was sometimes almost suicidal with rage. I once nearly threw myself from a seventeenth-floor penthouse window.

Why did I tell E about R? I needed the ballast of E's concern to keep from killing R, or myself, and I took it where I found it. "I think you're being set up," E said.

Why did I put myself through such conflict? I was mad with unexpressed love for E, and with R's ricocheting attention. I despaired of ever finding both love and sex in the same man. Even deeper lay sexual shame, from my father's violence toward my mother, and a religious education that said I couldn't be both sexual and good. I simply couldn't bring together these two sides of myself.

Now I snuggled closer to Porter. He stirred, opened his eyes, and looked deeply into mine. He reached for me, pulled my body against his. I could lie with his nearly naked body and kiss him all day, but that was as far as I wanted to go out there.

"I'm sorry," I said. Our love life was fine at home, and I thought it would be even better in our own Garden of Eden, days of intimate talk and romantic nights under the stars. But Adam and Eve didn't hike all day, only to crawl into camp hurting and dirty and scratching their mosquito bites.

Porter sighed and crawled out of our sleeping bag. He lit his homemade stove to make the mocha coffee I looked forward to each morning.

How could I explain that under the stress of physical and emotional survival, deeply buried conflicts were resurfacing? I sometimes dreamed of R and E.

"We need to talk about our sex life," I said.

"Sex under the tarp?"

For months before our hike, he ordered fabric and cords in various nylons and strengths, which he made into tarps of varying shapes, looking for the perfect mix of conjugal shelter and light weight. He worked hardest on our double sleeping bag, a custom-made down-filled top of water-resistant but breathable fabric, to which he zipped a Tyvek bottom. Our bedroom grew full of tarps and sleeping bags we could send for, in different sizes and weights depending on weather conditions.

"Sex anywhere," I said. "It's a normal part of life for you, like hiking, bicycling, skiing, mountaineering, and rock-climbing."

"You hike," he said.

He brought me my mocha coffee. We sat close together, passed our hot pot back and forth. We ate granola bars and wiped the crumbs from each other's mouths.

"Am I hiking to get sex?" It hit me like a ton of boulders. "All day I run after you down the trail, chasing you for sex."

He choked on his granola bar and sprayed us both with soggy crumbs. "I hadn't noticed." He brushed us off. "You don't want to make love when you catch me."

"I know. Why is that?"

"You're asking me?"

I was confusing us both by asking for sex I didn't want to have out there. I needed the reassurance of making love, but at the same time I just couldn't do it because of exhaustion and grunginess, not to mention the trail's way of baring old issues.

"Seduce me in spite of myself," I said in a burst of revelation. "I want to be ravished."

He sighed. "I won't force you if you don't want to."

Embarrassed by my need, I was annoyed at his response. "But I just realized the problem. Don't you want to solve it?"

"I don't see the problem."

"I know," I said. "That's the problem."

He jumped up and stuffed our sleeping bag into its sack.

We ascended and descended through the chaparral, fields of boulders, and jungles of willow, alder, and cottonwood. The path was hard to find. Theoretically, the Pacific Crest Trail was marked by the PCT emblem, a round-edged triangle on intermittent posts, as well as diamond-shaped metal nailed to tree trunks. Sometimes blazes were cut into or painted on tree bark, and rocks piled into cairns. Markers could be miles apart, or destroyed by loggers, bikers, wilderness purists, even animals. Occasionally all we could follow were boot prints made by hikers ahead.

But here an enormous mudslide had wiped out the trail. We stopped where it simply dropped off the edge.

"It's just—gone," I said.

He scanned the mountain across the gorge. "It picks up on the other side."

"How will we ever get there? There must have been an earthquake right *here*."

Porter dropped into the yawning crack between the eroded mudbanks.

"Where are you?" I cried over the edge.

"See the upended tree root at the very bottom?" he called back. "Aim for it and you'll be okay."

I couldn't see him, only hear him. I had no choice. I half-slid, half-threw myself down, down, into the roots far below. Now what? My pack straps, arms, even my legs, were caught in the muddy tangle. It was like fucking a tree.

"Wait right there," he called out again. "I'll climb out the other side, drop my pack at the top, and come back for yours so you can untangle yourself."

One way or another I'd die out here.

My father often came home drunk and beat up my mother in front of my brother and me. This was before women's shelters. One night, my mother went to the hospital, and my father went to jail. My father got out the next morning. My mother couldn't leave the hospital for several days, but when she did, one of the parish priests showed up at our house to counsel her. That's what they did; I'm sure my mother didn't invite him. The men raged, and the women were supposed to pray. My mother was furious. "What do priests know about marriage?" she said when he left. Was she asking me? I was seven.

Male drunkenness and violence were common in our parish, but the women and children kept it a shameful secret. My mother was too ashamed to tell her family, and my brother and I were taught not to tell a soul. I was terrified of everything—my father, other people knowing, making a wrong move myself and causing my mother more worry than she already had. Before reliable birth control, my mother got pregnant again. My little brother was born prematurely and nearly died. I set up an altar on a bookshelf in our hallway, and prayed as hard as I could. Baptized Mark, he lived, and became the one bright spot in our gloomy household. He was blond, with a sunny smile, inexplicably happy.

When I was eight, I began to take care of my one-year-old brother after school so my mother could go to work as a librarian.

I heated the milk for his bottle, changed his diaper, made sure he had his baby blanket and didn't fall off of anything. Two years later my mother managed to move us out of the house where we lived with my father, to a ground-level apartment in the housing project, where my father broke in by smashing his fist through the door glass. My mother ran to our phone, but before she could call the police, he tore the entire unit from the kitchen wall. I stared, terrified, at the tangle of wires—red and blue like veins.

One leg and arm at a time, I untangled myself from the tree roots.

Porter dropped his pack at the top and slid down to get mine. I began the long scramble up the muddy sides of the hole. Porter reached the top before me. I looked up and focused on him, his face in a blue field of sky.

Finally at the lip of the ravine, I reached and he tugged me out. We wrapped our arms around each other in relief.

"Let's eat our next installment of breakfast," he said.

I loved that he relished my rescue as cause for a celebratory snack.

I staggered around and searched for a spot to spread out my empty trash bag. Even filthy as I was, I didn't like to sit in the dirt, at bug-and-snake level. Porter leaned his back against his pack. When I tried that, my pack fell off a cliff. I'd prefer a chair and hassock, actually.

"Peanut butter?" I handed him the plastic jar.

He scooped it out in spoonfuls and slathered it on bread. "No way was that chasm in the guidebook."

I studied the indispensable pages from Schifrin, Schaffer, Winnett, and Jenkins's *Pacific Crest Trail: Southern California* over his shoulder. It was brilliantly detailed for hikers and equestrians, but I could only puzzle over terms of direction and orientation. "What's the difference between a saddle and a gap? Or a ridge line and a ridge crest? What's it mean, 'to a narrow gap in a saw-blade ridge of granodiorite needles'? You've got to be a frickin' geologist."

Not to mention a botanist and a meteorologist. If you failed to take the fork at the creosote bushes you might find yourself trapped at the bottom of a box canyon with pit vipers, or sleeping precisely on the San Andreas Fault. Even in town, with permission to camp in the park, you had to be careful not to get doused by a thunderstorm or by laying your sleeping bag on top of a sprinkler head.

"I've got to be a frickin' sexologist," Porter said.

"It's just that after each day of hiking twenty miles up and down the California mountains, my whole body has a headache."

"It's okay," he said.

A woodpecker pecked in the conifers, and a dark-eyed junco trilled its single pitch. Mountain bluebirds hovered and dropped to catch insects. Startled by a long *kra-a-a,* I looked up to the flashing white of a nutcracker's tail.

"No, it's not." It wasn't okay with me to be as conflicted as an adolescent, and it wasn't okay with him either, apparently, if he was still thinking about it.

"What do you expect me to say?" he said.

Why wasn't this the answer I wanted? Porter was of the "if it ain't broke, don't fix it" school of domestic life, where I believed "it's broke, but no one will admit it." I wanted it fixed and wouldn't rest until it was. At home, he insisted on doing household repairs to the point where I wouldn't tell him something was broken until I was ready to deal with the mess he'd make repairing it. He saw no problem with our sex life. Why was I in a whirling vortex of old sexual despair?

We followed muddy Mission Creek much of that day, and the gnats followed us, swarming our noses and mouths for moisture. My thoughts circled each other, buzzed in confusion. Did the same carefulness that made Porter and me excessively polite, for fear we'd take our problems with ourselves out on each other, make me wary of passion? You can be considerate during sex, you can be caring, but you can't hold back. I wanted waterfalls, not the slow channels of Mission Creek. But how could I surrender to passion, without scaring myself?

We stomped through lodgepole pine and juniper and descended through white-fir groves along Arrastre Creek. We hiked until after dark and pushed to make it to Arrastre Trail Camp, our last night out before resupply at Big Bear City, near Big Bear Lake.

"I wonder why it's called Big Bear," I said, then rounded a switchback and screamed.

The large dark shape ran toward us. Its eyes gleamed yellow in the dark. Should we defend ourselves or flee?

"Get the camera." Porter grabbed my arm.

"Are you crazy?"

But the creature was upon us—an enormous chocolate Labrador retriever. He jumped all over us. We petted him until he calmed down and followed us forlornly into the deserted camp.

"He's lost," Porter said.

I had a hard time getting reception on our satellite phone in the dense forest, but finally I was able to leave a message at the phone number on the dog's tag. "We have #1 Odin," I told them. How many Odins were there?

I longed to comfort him, hungry and cold. He hovered so close to Porter lighting our stove, we worried the dog would get burned.

"I'll make a deal with you, Odin," Porter said. "You wait over there, and I'll tell you when supper's ready."

He obliged.

"That is one really smart dog," I said.

His ears perked up when our phone rang, from a Los Angeles movie studio hours away. He'd wandered off from a compound at the top of the mountain with lions, tigers, bears, and dogs who performed in films. As #1 Odin, he was a superstar.

"Odin's like a son to me," his panicked owner said.

"Don't worry, we're taking good care of him," I said. "Is he allowed ramen noodles?"

The dog looked up hopefully when he'd finished his share.

"He's a movie star," I said to Porter. "He can have my food."

It was freezing, in the teens, but Odin was so valuable that the compound caretaker went out in a jeep to try to find us. Porter hiked in the pitch dark to hang a white T-shirt on a bush next to what he thought might be a dirt road. It was futile, deep as we were in the forest.

We bedded down, but at every sound, Odin ran to the edge of the clearing and stared into the darkness.

"Come over here with us, Odin," I begged. "Or none of us will get any sleep."

Shivering, he finally settled down at our heads. We covered him with our extra clothes. I wrapped one arm around him, and Porter wrapped his around me.

"When you want to talk about sex," Porter confessed, "I feel I must be doing something wrong, like I'm not good enough."

"You're way past good enough."

We snuggled deeper into our sleeping bag, and Odin nestled closer to us.

THRU-HIKERS IN TOWN

FROM MEXICO: 260 MILES. TO CANADA: 2,403 MILES.
At dawn, we shared the last of our food with Odin.

"We'll have to bushwhack to get him out." Porter studied the topographical map.

It was a bad idea to depart from the trail, but if anyone could find a road, he could.

"Odin," I said, "you'll need to stick with us."

The three of us set off. We loved hiking with this dog. He sniffed ahead with intelligence, good-naturedly loped behind. He gave me a sense of the trail as a continuous present, even as I revisited unresolved parts of my past and wondered what was to come.

Finally we scrambled out of the forest and emerged onto California's Highway 38. We called the compound caretaker on her cell and tried to describe the piece of highway we were on.

We were standing on the shoulder, Odin between Porter and me, when the caretaker appeared a half hour later. She had driven up and down the highway for hours, and shook with relief when she opened the car door for Odin.

"I've got him," she said into her cell phone to his owner in L.A.

She was too freaked out to thank us, but Odin hopped into the car, wagged his tail, turned, and smiled his doggy thanks.

"I miss him already," I said as they drove off.

We disappeared again into the forest, but it was impossible to find the trail by bushwhacking back. Rattled by the traffic, we walked the highway toward Big Bear City. It was hot, and we were hungry and out of food.

Porter was unhappy to be missing a part of the trail. I, on the other hand, was on my best behavior, for fear he'd stamp our zip code on my forehead and mail me back to Houston. In our first two weeks on the PCT, I'd managed to nearly die of hypothermia, fall over and over in snow, tear my shoulder muscle, get dehydrated, and bitch about sex.

"I love this," I said as we walked west.

"Where's Gail?" He looked around.

"I'm serious. I like hiking and camping, being filthy, mountain-climbing, snow, bugs, all that."

He put his hand on my forehead. "Are you sick?"

"It's just taken me time to get used to." The longer I stayed on the trail, the more invested I became in completing the whole six months. I had survived so much already. I was learning new outdoor skills every day. I'd learned something primal from Odin. He was lost and he surrendered, trusting us. I would trust where the trail was leading, trust myself.

"What happens when we face our next crisis?" Porter asked.

Here was my chance to be as patient with him as he was with me. It couldn't be easy to feel responsible for me and my safety. I appreciated him, after my old boyfriend who seemed not to care what happened to me.

A car pulled up in front of us on the shoulder, and a girl leaned out. "PCT hikers, right? Want a ride into Big Bear?"

Porter and I looked at each other.

"If we take it," he muttered to me, "we'll no longer be 'pure.'"

Pure was the term for hikers who hiked every one of the 2,663 miles. It was a badge of hiker honor, like being a wilderness virgin.

"It's a slippery slope," I agreed. "What's to keep us from doing it again?"

The girl waited patiently. "I know how you feel," she said out the window. "I've hiked sections, and someday I'll do the whole thing."

"On the other hand, my feet are killing me," Porter said.

"Get in the car," I said. "They have great sex in Big Bear."

Heather drove us the last few miles and dropped us off at a budget motel.

I closed our room's curtains. "I'm sorry for driving you crazy about our love life," I said. Everything in the wilderness—tongued flower and bee, throat-pumping lizard, seed in moist earth—sang with sex. "It's all sex out here."

We tore off our clothes. I inhaled his musk, earthy as the trail, and buried my face in his brushy chest. He was as solid as the trunk of a tree; I twined like a vine around him. I was all sun-dappled leafiness, he as lithe as a beast.

We were eager to see which other thru-hikers had made it into Big Bear. On the trail, hikers slipped by our tarp in the dark, or we slipped by them early morning while they were still asleep. No one approached another's tent unless invited. It would have been an invasion of privacy, of the solitude of their experience. And during the day, hikers approaching from behind were paragons of sensitivity and tact. They sang, they coughed, they whistled so as not to startle us. In general, we all moved along together, a nomadic tribe separated by only a few miles.

We easily recognized other thru-hikers in town, all of us doing the same errands—post office, grocery store. At the Laundromat, we were the ones naked under our raincoats, washing every stitch we had. We were all recognizable by gait, walking gingerly on sore feet. Even from a distance, we spotted one another by our clothes. Except for our foul-weather layers, we each wore pretty much one outfit. Porter and I were clearly a couple in our matching synthetic straw sunhats, nylon khaki pants, and long-sleeved shirts—mine light blue and Porter's gray. Tom and Sheila still looked as if on safari in their khaki hats, pants, and shirts with multiple pockets. The younger people were the least pulled together in their sweatshirts and sweatpants, T-shirts and cargo shorts, bandannas or wool caps pulled low over their ears. To the

Border Patrol, we were all distinguishable in our varying degrees of yuppie attire from the illegal immigrants, shirtless and toting trash bags in their threadbare jeans.

We could afford a motel room to ourselves, but thru-hikers with little money slept six to a double-occupancy room. Their door open for air, they hung damp sleeping bags and tents across makeshift clotheslines, then piled in a heap on the bed with pizza to watch cartoons. Those who couldn't afford to share a motel room sorted through their gear and food in a park or parking lot.

Now, outside the grocery store, a few young hikers went through their pockets and counted their change.

"We have to find a way to help buy food without embarrassing them," I said.

"I'll take care of it." He walked over and pretended to find a twenty on the ground. "This must be yours," he told them.

Relief spread across their faces.

On the trail, the kids had boundless energy, where we had high-tech lightweight gear. They had their youth, where we had monetary acorns from years of squirreling them away in the bank.

"I wish I'd hiked the Pacific Crest Trail in my twenties, before I started deferring my gratification," I said when Porter came back, "instead of dropping acid and acting wild on the streets of Chicago."

"That was the '60s," he said. "They didn't have a PCT then."

The Pacific Crest National Scenic Trail wasn't officially dedicated until June 5, 1993, although people had hiked and ridden horses on pieces of it long before that. In 1920, the Forest Service designated a route from Mount Hood to Crater Lake in Oregon the Oregon Skyline Trail. But it was a woman, Catherine Montgomery of Bellingham, Washington, who suggested in 1926 that there be a western mountain trail comparable to the Appalachian Trail in the east. It took a lot of effort, disputes, and agreements on the part of various regions of the Forest Service, the National Park Service, private property owners, and mountaineering and youth clubs to route and build the PCT of today.

We headed to the post office to sign the "trail register" with our names, the date, and a comment about the trail. We were Nos. 21 and 22, respectively, to sign the one at the Idyllwild post office a week before, out of about three hundred hikers who set out to thru-hike that season. We hoped to stay in this first wave as long as possible, to increase our chances of finishing in at least the middle of the pack. By Big Bear, we'd slipped just a little, to Nos. 25 and 26.

We scanned the register to see who'd been through and when, and whether they were still in town. It was a kind of message board.

"Tom and Sheila are here!" I said.

"Maybe we'll run into them at supper," Porter said.

The buzz up and down the PCT told us where to find the best breakfast, the biggest portions at lunch, and who had the cheapest all-you-can-eat dinner buffet. The servers in these towns were true trail angels who kept our coffee cups and water glasses filled, the pancakes and syrup coming. They were used to thru-hikers, and put up with separate checks. We tipped them lavishly.

A cheer went up when Porter and I walked into Big Bear's Pizza Kitchen that evening. Tom and Sheila were crammed into a booth with Zigzagger and Tangent. More hikers had acquired their trail-names by now.

They jumped up to give us bear hugs, and we hugged each in turn, all of us overjoyed we'd survived our ordeals thus far. It was in town that I most loved the trail, in the collective pride and camaraderie.

"How's your foot?" Tangent asked Porter.

"Better," Porter said. "And thanks for those directions to water."

Tangent, hiking lighter and faster than the rest of us, often went out of his way to check out off-trail water sources. He left a note under a rock on the trail for those of us behind. "Don't bother hiking a mile down to creek—dry." Or "Spring with good water two hundred yards south of trail, near ponderosa pine."

"Aren't these yours?" I handed Zigzagger the expensive sunglasses he had lost and we had found on the trail.

His jaw dropped. "Thanks. Didn't think I'd see those again."

We had last seen Zigzagger on our tortuous descent from Fuller Ridge, when we came upon him camouflaged against the dusty landscape, photographing a rattlesnake. At least six feet long, it rattled and hissed. We watched for several minutes from a safe distance, and with our zoom took a few photos of our own. "How'd you get that close?" we asked, once he released the snake from its photo-op. "Practice," he said. Sunburned and in his fifties, he was a wildlife conservationist and photographer. He traveled all over the world taking photographs for national magazines, and knew the name of every creature and plant we quizzed him about.

But human nature fascinated me more than animals and plants. I looked around the table, saw in the others' faces the ravages of traumas past and present. Their trail stories—of dehydration, getting lost, caught in storms—revealed their own struggles to come to terms with themselves.

"Anyone seen Leather Feet, Steve, and Kyle?" I asked.

"Steve and Kyle took off for a jazz festival in Palm Springs, and Leather Feet dropped back to look for Tender Heart," Zigzagger said. Zigzagger knew something about nearly everyone on the trail. He was our town crier. "I heard you had pasta with Pine Needle at the Pink Motel," he said to Porter and me.

As if on cue, Pine Needle showed up. We made room for him while Porter, Tom, Zigzagger, and Tangent all razzed him in a ritualistic male greeting.

"Where'd you get that great hat?" Porter asked Pine Needle.

"Found it in the hikers' box," he said.

The hikers' box was another piece of trail culture, usually a big cardboard carton near the trail register outside the post office. Hikers put into it whatever they didn't need, and were free to take what they wanted. After you repackaged in plastic bags what you bought at the store—dry milk, granola, a loaf of bread, panti-liners—you left any extra in the hikers' box. It even had cast-off gear—wool socks, gloves, shoes.

"Anyone heard the depth of the snowpack in the High Sierra?" Pine Needle asked.

We shook our heads no. The High Sierra was still hundreds of miles north, but we were all worried about it.

"How'd you do in the snow on Fuller Ridge?" I asked Sheila.

"I recognized your footprints," she said. "I said to Tom, if Gail can do it, so can I."

"I fell a lot," I said. "It was awful."

We marveled at all the ways there were to stumble, besides slip in snow. Sheila tended to stub her toes on rocks, where Tom tripped over roots. Porter tripped but caught himself, where I fell down. Sheila got teary with exhaustion, Tom cussed. I tended to cry, where Porter sank into stoic silence. We were all subject to "bonking," the kind of running out of steam that meant we had to eat.

"Isn't the wilderness beautiful, though?" I asked Sheila.

She agreed. Neither of us wanted to be anywhere else but here.

"You guys got trail names yet?" Tom asked Porter and me. "I'm 'Start Slow' and Sheila is 'Taper Off.'"

"No," Porter said. Even hikers we had yet to meet had trail names—Killa and Nachos, Leprechaun, Hawkeye, Cactass and Sycamore. Tough-Old-Broad, Snickers, Mountain Goat, One Gallon and Fritz. Radar, Data, Pi.

"How about Pippin and Merry, since you share 'the Hobbits' view about regular meals, plenty and often'?" Sheila said, quoting Tolkien.

True, most of the other hikers we met on the trail came upon us eating. Soon after our second installment of breakfast, we had our first installment of lunch, then lunch, then our last installment of lunch, followed by our first installment of supper.

"I want trail names with more gravitas," I said, "like 'Mountain Man' for Porter and something pretty for me like 'Gazelle.'" On the other hand, I would like to have been 'Trainwreck,' but it was already taken. I aspired to meet her, sure we were kindred spirits.

"How about 'Whines-a-Little' and 'Whines-a-Lot'?" Porter asked.

"No, and no."

In any case, trail names were more often given than chosen, reflecting your peers' opinion of your trail persona.

I was baffled to find myself a thru-hiker, united with the others on our trek from Mexico to Canada. They readily accepted discomfort as part of living in the wilderness. They valued closeness to nature, and free time more than money. They didn't care about status or control over other people. Of the rugged individualist species, thru-hikers were more rugged and individualist than most.

My legs and back were growing strong. I felt more open and soft, itself a kind of strength. But I was well aware that my shoulder injury and nocturnal leg twitching could do me in, physically and emotionally.

While the guys talked about their gear and respective paces, Sheila and I talked about our leg pains.

"Take some of these." She gave me a handful of pills, as if we were doing a drug deal.

Porter noticed, horrified.

"I'm desperate," I said. "If they work for Sheila, they'll work for me."

"Where'd you get them, Sheila?" Porter asked.

"From a pack of bikers."

Porter frowned.

"Way it happened was," Tom said to Porter, "a group of bicyclists found us collapsed by the roadhead, hitching into town. I was sick, and Sheila's feet and legs were killing her, so they took us to one of their homes for food and rest."

"They were triathletes," Sheila said, "with shelves of nutritional supplements."

Porter studied the pills. "B-complex vitamins, magnesium, and zinc."

"Since you're a doctor and Pine Needle's a pharmacist," Tom said, "why don't you two work out a way to prescribe medications for the rest of us with our gut problems, aches, and pains?"

"I'm not going there," Porter said.

"Me neither," Pine Needle said.

Porter and I walked back to our motel for the night, concerned that so many thru- hikers didn't have health insurance. They were between school and their first jobs, or just between jobs. We had health insurance, but Porter still agonized over what his next job would be.

"You're one of the top hospice and palliative care doctors in the country," I tried to reassure him. "Once you're done with this hike, hospices will line up for you."

Who would I be when I finished the trail, or the trail was finished with me? Out here in this spaciousness, I was growing beyond my old roles—my mother's worried daughter, my father's estranged one. Party girl, spiritual seeker, indignant daughter-in-law. Even with its disturbances, my old life felt cocoonlike, familiar. Now it was cracking, rough and scratchy against my inner edges. If I had to come up with trail-names for us, they'd be "Once-Porter" and "Once-Gail."

A RARE TOAD LIVES HERE

FROM MEXICO: 274 MILES. TO CANADA: 2,389 MILES.
The next morning, I called my mother before we hit the trail. She sounded more fragile this time, as if on her bedroom extension instead of standing at her kitchen phone. It was her nightgown voice, pale but etched with sharp sweetness.

But she told me she was fine. I told her I was fine.

"We're about to leave Big Bear," I said.

I waited while she marked it on her map. I felt a sudden urge to apologize for all I'd put her through, before it was too late.

"Mum," I said, "I'm sorry—"

"For what?" she interrupted.

She had sent me to a Catholic women's college outside Chicago because she thought it was best for me, but also because it would take me as far from my father's violence as possible. At the time, I felt like a bird pushed too soon from the nest, then blamed for learning to fly the wrong way. I went to New York University my junior year for an expanded curriculum, but I was even more out of my element in Greenwich Village than in a midwestern women's college. It was the late '60s, and I basically threw away my virginity on a smooth-talking street dude I hardly knew. "You flaunt sex," my mother said when I went braless and wore too much eye makeup. I was desperate to fit in with a sexual parade that seemed to be passing me by.

After that, my mother and I didn't know how to talk with each other. In my thirties, I began an arduous journey toward some sort of rapprochement, the terms of which I barely knew how to negotiate. My way back into my mother's good graces had been as long a trek as the PCT was miles.

"For everything I put you through—"

"Oh for Pete's sake," she said.

In childhood you want your parents' approval, in adolescence you viscerally don't, and in adulthood you do your own thing regardless. But out here on the trail, I saw that she and I were each shaped by forces—familial, sexual, and social—beyond our control.

"Should I take that as forgiveness?" I asked Porter when I got off the phone.

"Your mother is proud of you," he said. "You had to go through everything you did to be who you are today."

And who was that? Everything I thought settled about myself was being shaken up.

Porter called his mother, whose voice boomed with displeasure. From his perfunctory replies he sounded as if he were holding her at arm's length. I didn't want to take her side against Porter, but what forces shaped her? She could be difficult, but she gave birth to and raised my husband. She threw parties for us, gave us gifts, introduced us to her friends.

"Maybe you could sound a tad more understanding?" I said.

"She'd eat me alive."

"You don't have to agree with her. You could listen, then do whatever you want."

"What about my integrity?" he asked.

What could I say? A deeply ingrained honesty, with himself and other people, had always been part of who Porter was. It was why he stayed in his previous marriage for nine years, and why he finally left it, not to mention why he left his hospice job when it proved untenable. Integrity was why he was committed to hiking the whole PCT, and taking care of me.

Back on the trail early morning, we broke through thin filaments spun by spiders during the night. Shimmering blue and green, they seemed as tenuous as my phone connection with my mother. We were joined in mutual vulnerability, she in her illness, and I on the trail.

I took comfort in being part of the thru-hiker community—a band of vagabonds, a congregation, a sangha. We all moved at separate paces but as one—the kids, Pine Needle with his Bible, Zigzagger, Tangent, Tom and Sheila slow with their heavy packs, and we hardly faster with our lighter ones.

Midmorning, I spotted Sheila in the distance, her bright red rubber mallet swinging from the back of her pack.

"Oh, honey," I said when I caught up to her. "Your mallet must weigh two pounds."

"I need it to hammer in tent stakes."

I couldn't even pick up her pack. On the other hand, she and Tom lacked for nothing, unlike some of the kids whose heavy packs didn't have what they needed.

"We couldn't carry the pounds you do," Porter said.

"I never met a piece of gear I didn't like," Tom said. He even had a scooper to dig his cat-hole.

"He researched a ton of lightweight gear and bought it all," Sheila said.

We stopped at a creek too shallow to dunk our bottles.

"Here, use my dipper," Tom said.

I measured out the two parts of our Aqua Mira water treatment drops, seven of chlorine dioxide and seven of phosphoric acid activator, the only formulation available then, into a tiny cap. Sitting still so as not to knock over the cap as I'd done before, I waited the required five minutes for the chemical reaction. I poured it into one of our liter bottles and shook it to distribute it. After fifteen to thirty minutes, depending on how cold or turbid the water, it would be safe to drink. Each liter had to be treated this way. We didn't carry a water filter; they were heavier than drops and clogged in what silty water we found.

"Got any more Aqua Mira?" I asked Porter, since we still had several bottles to treat. We each carried drops in our packs in case we got separated. Water was so crucial to survival, we planned much of our day around finding it, carrying it, camping near it, and especially treating it.

But Porter was also out. We needed much more water than we'd imagined.

"Here, take some of ours." Tom handed me two tiny bottles with the two parts of the solution.

"We couldn't possibly," I said. Aqua Mira on the trail was like gold.

Porter was mortified, but we had no choice. "Thanks, Tom."

Porter got on our satellite phone to Colleen, our resupply friend in Houston, so she'd get on the Internet to our Aqua Mira supplier in New Hampshire, who'd FedEx it to our next town. It hadn't yet been approved in California.

"Want to call anyone on our phone?" Porter asked Tom and Sheila. He was eager to return the favor.

They shook their heads no, and the four of us set out again. While I gabbed with Sheila, Porter talked with Tom, or rather Tom talked. Porter wasn't one for talking while he hiked, one reason I had my chatting emergencies. When it was Porter's turn to lead, he dashed ahead, and I had to work to keep up with him. Soon we left Tom and Sheila behind.

"Sheila met Tom when she was nineteen," I said as I ran after Porter. "He was quite a bit older, but she fell for him. He was dating someone else, but Sheila bided her time. Her parents weren't pleased, but they came around when they saw what a great guy he was and how much she loved him. She comes from a big family and she's a twin. She and Tom are Protestants, but not fundamentalists. Sheila lost eighty pounds before this hike, with fifty more to go. Maybe that's why she doesn't mind carrying so much. Tom lost thirty, but he wants to lose another ten. Tom freeze-dried all their hiking food." I filled in Porter on all of Sheila's brothers and sisters and parents—where they lived and what they did.

He was aghast. "You should have been a psychotherapist."

"I'm fascinated by people," I said, "especially hikers our age. What'd you find out from Tom?"

"He got a lot of gear from REI."

Once again I was out there with strong, but mostly silent, Porter. On the other hand, I'd been so social most of my life, I found it a relief not to respond to everyone else's talk, needs, and concerns. Talk was the main way I connected with people, but it could be exhausting. Porter didn't require much responding. He was happy if I basically kept quiet.

Having talked more over the last two days than I had in two weeks, I was ready to calm down and listen to the natural world happening all around me. I wanted to fully experience each moment, pay attention to the rocky trail and blue sky. Sometimes I remembered where I was, in the mountains. But mostly I forgot, stuck in my own Cartesian chatter. I obsess, therefore I am.

My thoughts were a nuisance running over every available surface of my brain, jumping from neuron to neuron, nibbling away at my serenity. Every thought I ever had, every memory stuffed into the back of my mind, now popped up unpredictably. I wanted the wilderness to make such claims on my body that my thoughts would settle like silt on the bottom of a lake.

Porter obsessed too, now about running out of water treatment drops. "I worked so hard to prepare."

"We can't prepare for everything," I said.

But for him, being prepared was part of being competent, a good provider. He compulsively shopped for outdoor clothing, gear, and the materials to make them. At home, he had ten bicycling jerseys, nine tarps and tents, eight pocketknives, seven sleeping bags, six backpacks, five bicycling shorts, four pairs of running shoes, three pairs of skis, and two bicycles. I couldn't think of anything he had one of but me.

My own compulsion was organizing. Cleaning was a close second; the world was a dusty place. There was nothing worse than cleaning the house until it was spotless, only to watch dust in the sunlight settle immediately over everything. Organizing lasted longer than cleaning. Porter tried not to move things too much, because he wanted my satisfaction to last.

I knew my excessive neatness sprang from inner chaos, so at home I indulged it only on weekends. By Wednesday, when our household began to tilt out of place, I gave myself a pep talk. "Just a few more days, until Saturday, to let myself clean up the clutter," I told myself out loud. "Is that so hard?"

But there was nothing for me to organize out here. I reorganized my pitiful pile of gear in the compartments of my pack, but then I would come to the end of it. All that was left was to check and recheck that my lip balm was in the left front zippered pocket of my pack-belt, my antiseptic wipes in the right. My water bottle was in the right net pocket of my pack, and my snacks were in the left.

Once in a while, I looked at a forest and thought: someone should come in and clean up all these dead trees, trim the bushes, and vacuum the decaying duff from the forest floor. It looked, well, messy.

Nor was there anything out here for Porter to buy. He was forced to enjoy all the gear he bought. He'd be happier buying new, but could only tweak our clothes, packs, and stove.

When Porter wasn't obsessing about gear or the hospice, his inner life tended toward the ecstatic. He wrote in his journal as if talking with God:

May 4/This morning made love, packed up, bought white cotton gloves in Big Bear for sun protection, big breakfast, repaired gaiter. Hiked with Tom and Sheila. We're incredibly blessed to be here. Watch over us, we need all the help we can get. I'm Alive. I'm really Living!

My journal reads, on the other hand:

May 4/What the fuck am I doing here?

Even more than buying and organizing, Porter and I liked to accomplish things. Our favorite thing to do was to get things done. But there was nothing to get done on the trail except keep going.

On our arid trek toward California's Cajon Pass, we came upon the Mojave River Forks Reservoir's dam. Surprisingly, there was no water on either side. On the huge expanse of the dam's dry concrete, a small board exhibit read "A Rare Toad Lives Here."

Sometimes I felt at home out here, other times as vulnerable on this bare landscape as the endangered arroyo southwestern toad. I followed Porter across the spillway where an overgrowth of nettle and foxtails obliterated the trail.

After many dry but breathtaking miles across razorback ridges and down into cottonwoods, baccharises, and willows, we arrived beneath the cloverleaf interchange of Route 138 and six-lane Interstate 15 in Cajon Canyon. We hiked up the frontage road to gorge ourselves on burgers and chocolate milkshakes at a McDonald's, then stocked up on candy bars and snacks at a convenience store.

"I could never hike that trail." The young cashier popped her gum. "I get bored too easy."

"Bored?" Porter said when we burst out the door.

Nothing boring about our daily, even hourly, struggle for survival. Not to mention I was already anxious about tomorrow's steep climb up the snow-covered trails of Mount Baden-Powell.

We bought cherries at a roadside stand from a woman encircled by tiny kids who hid behind her skirts. She seemed Mother Earth herself.

"Come to our Tabernacle Church," she said when we told her we were hiking the trail. "Jus' come as you are."

"There's a lot of God out here," I said.

"Yes," she said. "God is big!"

A VISION QUEST?

FROM MEXICO: 378 MILES. TO CANADA: 2,285 MILES.

We descended back to the trail, and as if down a rabbit hole, into a dank tunnel beneath tracks of the Atchison-Topeka and Santa Fe Railroad. Trains rumbled overhead; graffiti demons glared from the vibrating walls. Moving small and hidden underground gave us a chill.

Our eyes had barely adjusted to the eerie blackness when a dark figure entered the tunnel from the other end. Far away at first, his silhouette loomed larger with each step. I felt the menace in his hunch. My heart pounded. We were too deep in the tunnel to turn back. Closer and closer, he approached. Porter slipped to my other side to put himself between me and this stranger.

His face shrouded by his hooded sweatshirt, he was almost upon us. Fear pressed on me like the tunnel walls. He was sizing us up when Porter nodded in greeting. He was as afraid of us as we of him. The man nodded curtly back. His shoulder brushed Porter's as we passed by. The darkness itself seemed to melt in relief.

Still shaken, we exited the tunnel and gawked at our next steep climb. The San Gabriel Mountains rose impossibly high on every side. The San Andreas Fault system rearranged the mountains several hundred miles at a geologic pop. The San Fernando Earthquake of 1971 alone had lifted them six feet. Treading Mesozoic granite rocks and the schist of volcanic and ocean-bottom sediments, we could almost feel the earth's heaving motion.

Twenty miles later, high in the San Gabriels, we left the brushy chaparral of sagebrush and pink-blooming manzanita, mountain lilac and chamise, for white fir and Jeffrey pine. Partway up Mount Baden-Powell, we camped for the night on a narrow ledge, the only flat spot we found. The sky flamed orange and crimson before deepening into night.

His back pressed against the mountain, Porter cooked our dinner. At home, I did all the cooking—tikka masala, pasta puttanesca, cauliflower marranca. On the trail I simply collected and treated water, helped as sous-chef.

"When did you learn to cook outdoors?" I asked.

"As a teenager at a survival camp. My first night alone in the woods, I had to kill a rattlesnake for dinner."

"Yuck." I was horrified, but glad to be out here with a man who could do that if he had to.

"But it's Pan-Asian fusion tonight," he said, "lo mein noodles in a lemongrass, soy, and teriyaki sauce with ginger-seasoned Thai vegetables."

"One of your best dinners yet," I said as we ate straight from the pot.

"Getting enough?" He was torn between love and hunger, capable of eating the entire dinner by himself.

We had run out of food on one of our first days on the trail, before we knew how much we'd eat. Hungry and anxious, we jogged to our next supply stop. Why not carry more food, so there was no question of enough? It was a catch-22—the more you carried, the slower you went. The slower you went, the longer it took to get there, and the more food you had to carry. Your objective was to come into town with little, if anything, left over.

"The rest is yours," Porter said now as we neared the bottom of our pot.

"I'm done."

"Just one more bite."

"I can't," I said.

"You sure?" He scraped the inside of the pot clean with his spork and poured in a little water. He cleaned the pot further with his finger, then drank the water.

I couldn't bear to do that, or even watch, but water was so scarce we couldn't waste a drop.

I circled around myself like a cat until I found a narrow space to lay out our sleeping pads on the edge of this sheer drop-off. I shuddered at its plunging depth. How narrow the space of our daily lives, how close the ledge of death.

We crawled into our sleeping bag.

I threw one arm over Porter and held him close. "Let's not roll off the ledge."

In the morning, we ate our breakfast, packed up, and continued our ascent. By 8,000 feet, we were switchbacking tightly among lodgepole pines.

But by 9,000 feet, a ferocious cold wind sprang up on the snow-covered trails. In just a couple of hours, we'd hiked from summer to winter. Time and distance grew stranger by the day, and now the seasons too. The trail was a shape-shifter; we couldn't hold on to a sense of what to expect from it. We lost the trail under icy fields of last winter's snow that hadn't yet melted under the pines.

"We'll have to bushwhack straight up the mountainside," Porter shouted above the roar.

For the next two miles I did my best to follow, hauled myself up the sharp slope by grasping at the gnarled trunks of 2,000-year-old limber pines, bent into weird shapes by the wind. Soon the trees thinned out, and flattened by my backpack, I crawled on my belly up the scree.

But the loose rock was too steep, and after a while I was exhausted, slipping down two feet for each one I advanced. I collapsed on the rockslide. Sharp-edged stones dug into my face. Heaving with sobs, I slid further down the slope.

"I can't. I can't." The wind took away my cry.

Porter scrambled down to stop my slide, his face a mix of disappointment and fear.

"I hate this," I sobbed. "Shit. Damn it."

He tugged and pushed whatever he could—my arm, foot, butt, until we made the top at 9,245 feet. At the highest point on the PCT in Southern California, I was at my lowest morale.

We began our descent through Windy Gap. Hours later, we dropped off the ridge to fill up on water at Little Jimmy Spring.

We had hoped to camp a few minutes further up the trail at Little Jimmy Campground, with its picnic tables and fire pit among the pines. But it was so windy there we could barely stand. Porter cooked a hot meal of black beans and rice with salsa. We crouched under a picnic table to eat.

"Too windy to camp here," he muttered.

I was wiped out, but relieved. I'd heard that a thru-hiker lost all his food to a bear here, which reached into his tent and pulled his bag from under his head.

We leaned into the wind and pushed on for miles to the summit of Mount Williamson. We set up camp in a small piney enclave. Porter kneaded dough with Parmesan and apricots in a plastic bag, then baked a large, round bread over his one-ounce homemade steamer. He was learning to bake at high altitudes, to prepare for the High Sierra ahead where there were a lot of bears. We would have to carry more food in powder form to compress into a three-pound bear canister.

"Your cheese-bread is good," I said. I was calm now, having climbed Mount Baden-Powell 2,660 feet up, then 2,575 feet down, then up to the top of Mount Williamson.

But Porter's mood blackened as we took turns sipping from a hot pot of chai. He stared out at the vastness and down into Devils Punchbowl, the southwest slash of the San Andreas Fault.

"You okay?" I asked.

He was silent a long time. "I'm sorry I brought you on this torture-fest," he said after a while.

I wanted him to say he was fine, and that I would be too. "It's not your fault, it's just a hard trail," I said. "I'm sorry I'm not more up to it."

He shrugged and looked out at the emptiness.

I gazed out too at this old, sad territory. I had enough grief, rage, even joie de vivre, for both of us. I was tired of myself. It was harder to endure than my slide down the rocky scree, slipping in snow, withstanding the wind. Shouldn't we be able to comfort each other, instead of isolating ourselves in separate shrouds of guilt?

Over the next hour or so, I reflected on our earliest days together. The conventional wisdom was that it took two years to get over a divorce. But Porter and I couldn't wait that long for him to recover from his, and got married a few months after the divorce was final. I was so conflicted about my own conflicts, I was willing to take on someone else's for a while. I took him with his barely repressed anger at his ex-wife, who had many of his mother's traits, and he took me with my fits. I had an Irish temper and a biting tongue that would make a sailor cringe, never mind a sensitive man like Porter. I pitched a fit whenever I felt him distance himself from me, a distance that panicked me like my mother's. My anger made him distance himself further, afraid he was repeating the dramas he'd had with his mother and ex-wife.

I was so afraid we wouldn't be able to extricate ourselves from this maelstrom, I consulted a psychotherapist. "He said I was too expensive to fix," I told Porter.

"I doubt he meant that," he said. "What did he say, exactly?"

"Group therapy is cheaper. But the only group he has now is a couples group."

He sighed.

Our group met in a cozy sitting room at the office of the therapist, who insisted we call him Bob. Bob looked more like an insurance salesman than a psychotherapist, which I found reassuring. He had a round face, neatly parted hair, and shined shoes, instead of the glazed look of shrinks in suede Hush Puppies who looked like they went home and tore their hair out.

Few things are as instructive as watching other couples fight, mainly over one of three things. Liz and Louis fought about money, Mary and Barry about their kids. Porter and I fought about sex, or rather, intimacy issues from our respective pasts. Bob said each couple's problems sprang from fights for power and control. Psychotherapy taught Porter and me that we were on the same side. In the end, we saw it as an extension of our education. It interested us; we were fascinated by the possibilities for emotional growth.

Finally Porter spoke. "How will we manage a month from now at 11,000 feet in the snow of the High Sierra?"

"I'll be a stronger hiker by then."

"Those slopes are steep and slippery, a lot worse than what we've come through. I can push you up rocky scree, but I'm worried."

"So what are you saying?"

"You'll have to decide if you're up to it," he said. "Yourself."

He kicked a stone over the edge of the cliff. I listened to it bounce all the way down, my heart plummeting.

"I can't give up. I gave up on the Appalachian Trail." I was despondent after Porter continued on the AT without me. We'd rented out our house to bike on our tandem to Maine, then hike the AT, so I had no place to go home to. With nowhere to go, I had everywhere to go, I fought to convince myself. Over the next two months, I took a journey of my own, parallel to Porter's, crashing with friends and friends of friends, finding my way to remote trailheads to provide him with moral support and resupplies. Day after day, I stood alone at various pay phones, calling for bus and train schedules and rental car rates. I felt homeless, heartsick with a failure I was desperate not to repeat.

"Yeah, I know," Porter said. "What would I do if I gave up? Admit defeat and look for a job?" Shoulders hunched, he stared into the darkness.

"Do you have doubts about completing the trail?"

"Sometimes," he said. "Why did I think slogging uphill with a heavy pack for six months would be fun? But it's not for fun, it's a vision quest. Whatever happens is part of it. I'll get to Canada or not."

A vision quest?

BLOWING AWAY

FROM MEXICO: 388 MILES. TO CANADA: 2,275 MILES.
That night at the summit of Southern California's Mount Williamson, bone-freezing gusts whirled over us. How could there be so much wind? It changed direction in the middle of the night and roared into our sleeping bag. We pulled the bag around our shoulders, but were still so cold we couldn't get back to sleep.

Porter scrambled out to rotate our bag, Blueberry. My weight—now only one hundred twenty pounds—wasn't enough to hold it down. The sleeping bag ballooned with wind and blew, with me inside it, across the mountaintop.

"Jesus," I screamed.

Porter chased me, a rolling purple worm, and threw himself on top. He dragged me out and held on to me and the bag whipping around us.

"We've got to get off the mountain," he shouted.

We fought the gale back to our campsite and grabbed our stuff to keep it from flying away. We lost track of what belonged to whom, just crammed what was at hand into our packs.

Pushed by the wind, we headed down the mountain. We were freezing, even in layers of our clothes. The wind made our eyes tear, and the cold crusted the tears into ice on our cheeks.

In the night's blackness, I couldn't find purchase with the tips of my trekking poles. They jabbed at the air, fell from my grip and dangled by the straps from my wrists.

My hands were so cold I couldn't feel them, until Porter stopped and warmed them in his armpits.

For hours we rounded switchback after switchback in a long descent of 2,260 feet, until we were finally out of the wind. We collapsed by Little Rock Creek and waited silently for dawn.

We'd also been blown away nineteen years ago, camping on a meditation retreat on a farm in Texas. It was dark by the time we found the farm down a long dirt road, and the other retreatants were already asleep in the bunkhouse. So as not to disturb them, Porter had brought a tent for us—a big geodesic dome.

I followed him into the field. A horse snorted and neighed. Porter stomped down the thick grass to make a spot to pitch the tent. With my flashlight, I searched the ground for fire ant mounds. Out in the country, there were supposed to be wildflowers in the spring, crickets in the summer, and a harvest moon in the fall. But I'd been in Texas long enough to know there were fire ants year-round, chiggers in the summer, and, it turned out, prickly cockleburs in the fall.

Porter spread out the tent. I got on my knees to help, but sprang up when the sharp, sticky burs pierced my sweatpants. All kinds of unseen things flew into me—bugs, even bats for all I knew. I sprayed myself with insect repellent to get ready for a night of being attacked by whatever lay in wait for me.

The tent rose. I had never spent a night in a tent. We spread out our sleeping bags. I followed Porter's lead of backing into the tent butt first, feet outside, taking off my shoes and picking off the burs. I lined up my stuff on my side of the dome—duffle of clothes, box of tissues, pink-frosted cupcakes, and a Diet Coke.

In the middle of the night, I woke up to rain pelting the tent. The howling wind lifted the bottom edges of the dome and blew the sides in and out like bellows.

"I guess I should have brought tent stakes," Porter said.

We fought to hold up the tent sides with our backs, the floor down with our legs.

I shared my cupcakes with Porter. Anxious as I was, I ate four of the six myself.

"I'm going to go sleep in the meditation hall," I said.

"If you go," he said, "my weight alone won't hold down the dome. The tent and all our stuff will blow across the farm."

But I was outta there. I raced in the wind and rain to the car with our duffels, while he struggled to hold on to the tent. Frantically we took it down and stashed it in the trunk. We ran to the meditation hall, a large wooden structure with a tin roof. The planked floor was covered with empty *zabutons* and *zafus*—pads and sitting cushions. We lay down together in the only empty space, on a small prayer rug at the front meant for the meditation teacher. Wrapped in each other's arms, we fell asleep.

We slept through the gong for the predawn meditation. I woke up feeling watched. I opened my eyes, looked straight up at the meditation teacher in lotus pose. The fluorescent Buddhist symbol on his T-shirt glowed.

"Holy shit," I said, which woke up Porter.

The meditation hall was packed with the retreatants. To their repressed snorts, we sat up cross-legged to begin our meditation.

At Little Rock Creek, beneath Mount Williamson, dawn brightened into morning. We set off on the Burkhart Trail to the Copper Canyon Trail, ascended a few hundred feet to Cloudburst Summit, descended to Cloudburst Canyon. We crossed the Angeles Crest Highway as morning radiated into high noon, noon into afternoon, the landscape hotter and drier the lower we went. Our descent from 6,000 to 2,300 feet was so steep, we hadn't found a flat spot to sleep on by early evening. The air cooled and the light changed from white to an amber glow. The sand turned pink, the pungent sage from gray to purple and green. The smallest trailside flowers cast long shadows as the sun sank behind the mountains.

By dark, we neared the bottom of Soledad Canyon, where we

would surely find a place to camp. But we stopped short when we rounded a switchback and found ourselves staring down into an RV campground. It was hard to believe the small figures below could make so much noise. Men shouted, women laughed, dogs barked, kids shrieked and ran.

"Let's just camp up here." I couldn't bear to disrupt our solitude by setting up camp on a hard RV site in the midst of exhaust fumes, blaring radios and TVs.

"We've got to be quiet," Porter said. "We don't want hunters with shotguns following their dogs up here, thinking they're on the trail of bobcats."

We had to break our rule not to camp on the trail itself, the only spot not covered with thorny brush. With barely room for both of us on the narrow path, we lodged rocks at our feet to keep from sliding down the slope.

"What if a hiker comes down the trail?" I asked. It was so hot at this lower altitude, a few walked at night and slept midday.

"Hopefully they'll see us in time to step over us," he said.

We fell asleep to the whistle of a train far below.

At the Buddhist retreat on the farm in Texas, the bell rang to end the dawn meditation. Thirty of us padded the path that led to the dining hall. In silence, we each chose a bowl, a cup, and utensils from the dish shelves. We ladled hot oatmeal into our bowls and added yogurt, honey, and raisins. We sat on benches at long wooden tables and cupped our hands around steaming cups of tea to watch the sun rise over the meadow. No one spoke, no one needed to. Even eye contact was discouraged, so as not to disturb anyone's inner solitude.

Life at the retreat, like life on the Pacific Crest Trail, was simple and obvious, even with their respective challenges. Porter and I signed the list on the bulletin board for a "yogi job," our chore for the communal weekend. A veggie chopper, I scrubbed my hands and stood at the butcher-block island to await instructions. The volunteer cook placed twenty pounds of raw carrots in front of me, silently demonstrated the size to slice them. I picked up a knife and started chopping.

Out of the corner of my eye I saw Porter at the sink, his big arms scrubbing at oatmeal stuck to the bottom of an enormous pot. Around me I heard the rustle of the other veggie choppers, and from my lowered eyes saw splashes of color—green broccoli, purple cabbage, red tomatoes, yellow peppers. I became absorbed in the rough texture of each carrot's skin as I held it with my fingertips, the soft whoosh of the knife, the brilliant orange of the wet slices.

After an hour, the person whose job it was rang the gong for the next meditation. We streamed from the kitchen, the bunkhouse, and the fields and slipped off our shoes at the entrance to the hall. The teacher gave a few instructions on mindfulness practice—to pay attention to whatever arose, whether breath, physical sensation, feelings, or thoughts, letting one go as another appeared. It was a challenging effort at effortlessness.

We passed the morning like this, alternating sitting and walking meditation hour by hour. Some people walked a few paces back and forth on the porch. Others struck out across the fields. I caught a glimpse of Porter, almost hidden in a thick patch of bamboo: lifting, moving, placing one foot at a time. I set off down the dirt road we'd come in on. I too lifted, moved, and placed each foot, but I was restless. I wanted to keep going, out the gate to wherever the road might lead.

Before dawn the next morning on the trail, we trekked down to the floor of Soledad Canyon, past the sleeping RV campers and along the railroad tracks. Among nesting mallards and blue herons, we forded the Santa Clara River, then strode up brushy mountainsides as the day heated up. Safely delivered from the wind on Mount Williamson, our hike felt almost blissful.

"I can see where this could be fun," I said, "out all day in the sun and breeze, with all these pink and yellow flowers, butterflies, and what-not."

"What-not?"

"It's so immediate. We're really here, in the so-called present moment."

The day on Porter's digital watch seemed to read *NOW*, until we realized it was *MON*, for Monday, upside-down. What did it mean to live in the present? Not to rush toward Canada the way we rushed through our lives. Nor could we amble and hope to get there. We would walk our miles as consciously as possible.

But with no crisis at hand, we grew preoccupied. I studied thoughts flying in out of nowhere. *What if . . .* I began so many. *I wish I had . . .* I quantified everything—*how many miles, what time is it, how long will it take to get there?*

Just as I wouldn't know enlightenment if it came up and hit me on the head, I still didn't know why I was there. But as with meditation, I knew something was happening to me on the trail, without knowing exactly what. Is that what Porter meant by a vision quest?

But he was back to obsessing on his next job. "As the baby-boomers die off," he said, "we'll need hospice doctors, right?"

"You're board-certified in internal medicine, geriatrics, and hospice and palliative care," I said. "Boomers will be banging down your door."

"Do you think they'll retire in places we'd like to live?"

"Worst-case scenario, we'll buy into an assisted living place in say, Santa Fe or Santa Barbara, you as the doctor and me teaching the residents how to 'tell their stories.' By the time we're old and decrepit, we'll be so dug in we won't have to move further than from skilled nursing to acute care."

"Oregon, maybe?" he asked. "Colorado?"

"Do we have to decide right now?"

The Pacific Crest Trail had been his escape fantasy for so many years I couldn't believe he was obsessing on work and where we would live. I worked so hard on being here now, I couldn't think of being there then.

I brought myself back to our mountain paradise of forest, fuchsia flowers, blue sky. In spite of the increasing speed of my emotional ascents and descents, I wanted to be here, really here. If my mind rambled on, so did the chatter of the songbirds.

We camped that night among young pines, sunset flaming through the green-needled branches. From our sleeping bag, we watched a robin circle the perimeter of our campsite and hop, rock to rock, to stare at us.

In the morning, I awoke out of sorts. I'd slept even worse than usual, shoulder and quadriceps shooting with pain. Porter tried to comfort me while he cooked us a frittata from egg powder and rehydrated vegetables. I was determined not to complain, but my grief widened in circles, from my own pain to everything wrong in the world.

"I'm ruining your hike. My mother's dying of cancer. People are at war."

"Gosh," he said.

"Sucks to be me."

Silently, he plied me with the frittata. We ate and set off.

We climbed until our descent into the dry wash of Bobcat Canyon. I switchbacked up and down my feelings, until they flattened out at the bottom of Escondido Canyon, where the sycamore trees were comforting presences, trunks white against the bloodshot bluffs. Among the yellow lichens and yerba santa, my dark thoughts shrank to mere nuisances, like the tiny gnats that swarmed before my eyes.

"Why don't you rest a few days in Agua Dulce," Porter said, "then catch a ride to meet me after I've hiked to Tehachapi."

"I can't miss the Mojave Desert."

"I'm frustrated with our slow pace and my heavy pack," he said. "It's so hard for you, and—"

And what?

He faced me. "Actually, I could use some time alone."

We had stopped beneath a precipice, the hot pink sandstone and purple cliffs of the Vasquez Rocks. I felt the weight of the massive overhangs, the 1850s hideout of outlaw Tiburcio Vasquez. The sharp, steep sediments were as layered as our feelings.

An enormous owl flew out and over us. I shrieked. The power of it was more than I could take in. Like Porter's revelations, flying out of the silence. Out here, just the two of us in the vastness, every nuance of feeling had more effect on the other than we intended.

"I want to stay on," I said.

We watched the owl soar away. Its wings took up the whole sky, then flapped smaller and darker until they sank into the emptiness.

"You freak at even the good stuff," Porter said.

How could I explain how the trail both opened me up and wore me down? I was raw inside, hypersensitive to good as much as to bad. He'd hiked long trails before, didn't he know they gave and took away?

The meditation retreat was as hard for Porter as the trail was now for me. He found it next to impossible to sit motionless through hour after hour of meditation. It cramped his long legs, his broad shoulders and back. Walking meditation wasn't much easier, with its speeds of slow, slower, and slowest. During the rest period, after lunch, most of us retired to the bunkhouse to nap. Porter ran the entire perimeter of the farm, then took his soggy tent from the trunk of the car, shook it out, and hung it to dry on the pasture fence. He looked for jobs that needed doing, and without being asked cleaned leaves from the gutters and swept the floor of the men's outhouse.

He was physically restless, and I was spiritually so. I read and reread the hand-lettered schedule nailed to the meditation hall's creaky door: *Sit, Breakfast, Work. Sit, Walk, Sit, Walk, Sit, Walk, Lunch, Rest. Sit, Walk, Sit, Walk, Sit, Walk, Tea.* Each activity had a time next to it, starting at 5:00 AM and ending at 9:00 PM, but we would have done just fine without it. All we had to do was the next thing. Sometimes a group of us huddled in front of the schedule, as though if we stared at it long enough, it would tell us the key to enlightenment.

We had tea and a snack around 5:00 PM. This nearly killed me, not because I needed more food, but Porter did. He pawed the ground with his feet before the door to the dining hall opened. He piled his plate with puffed rice cakes, as filling as Buddhist communion wafers. The poor guy, six feet two inches and one hundred eighty pounds with his mountain-man metabolism, was starving, and my heart ached for him. I wanted to feed him and take care of him as, years later, he'd want to take care of me on the Pacific Crest Trail.

After tea, we took the path back to the meditation hall for more sitting and walking. The sky brightened in contrast to the earth, glowed blue over the darkening farm. The teacher gave an evening dharma talk, about aspects of mindfulness practice: impermanence, resistance, patience, loving-kindness.

Now I lay in our sleeping bag with a new worry, the danger I was putting us in—not just myself, but Porter. I didn't know what to expect in the High Sierra, or even tomorrow. My abilities both amazed and disappointed me.

As thick as fireflies on the farm in Texas, the stars beamed hot and bright. So many, they pelted us from the sky.

HIKER HEAVEN

FROM MEXICO: 454 MILES. TO CANADA: 2,209 MILES.
We'd been on the trail for nearly five weeks. I was upset that Porter wanted time to hike alone. On one hand, I didn't blame him. On the other, this was my only chance to hike the PCT.

We walked west along Escondido Canyon Road, then turned north onto paved Agua Dulce Canyon Road into the small ranching town of Agua Dulce. The village had a few places to eat, a feed and supply store, and a market with a banner reading "Welcome, PCT Hikers." It was one of the few towns the PCT actually passed through, but had no motel for thru-hikers to clean up and regroup before facing the waterless Mojave Desert. Struck with compassion for a few exhausted hikers in 1997, Jeff and Donna Saufley invited them to spend the night, and had hosted thru-hikers ever since.

We walked into their compound, called Hiker Heaven, blooming with fruit trees. Dogs barked in welcome and nipped and sniffed at our shoes.

Donna met us at the door of the open garage. "The others said you were coming." Trim in jeans and a white jersey, she transferred laundry from her washer to her dryer. "Pick out something to wear while I wash your things." She pointed to a rack of clean clothes.

I was horrified. "I'll wash our clothes."

She grinned. "Sleep in our guest house, borrow our cars. Cook in the kitchen and make yourselves at home. Just don't get between me and my washing machine."

I chose a gauzy blue dress from the rack, Porter clean shorts and a shirt.

Donna's husband, Jeff, appeared, as kind and affable as she. "Storey?" He searched shelves of boxes for resupplies we'd shipped there. "Here you go."

Donna led us to her guesthouse, a doublewide trailer, to get us settled in one of the private bedrooms she reserved for couples. Single hikers had their choice of large and small tents set up under the trees. We showered in a real bathroom, with a real tub and toilet, shampoo, soap, and clean towels.

We weighed ourselves for the first time since we started the trail. "I've lost five pounds in five weeks," I told Porter.

"At 7,000 calories a day, five times what you eat at home?" he said. "At that rate you won't have the strength to stay on."

I bristled at this new tactic to get me to leave the trail. "What about you?"

"I've stayed about the same."

We emerged from the trailer in our borrowed clothes. In the filmy dress I felt light, even insubstantial. We joined a circle of thru-hikers lounging outside. They were a festive group, even attending to their blistered feet and worn gear.

"Hey, Porter-and-Gail," Zigzagger called out.

We were hiker Nos. 43 and 44 to sign the Saufleys' trail-register, out of the few hundred who'd come through this season. The DAMnations were there, three boisterous guys collectively trail-named because their first names began with D, A, and M respectively. And Jason and Snake Charmer, Garlic Man and Greasepot, Sisu and Raru, Lord Tea, Kent and Cathy.

Both of us tense about Porter's wish to hike alone and mine to stay with him, we didn't take part in the banter. We went to our room in the early evening, and in the confined space puttered over our respective piles of gear. Donna had delivered our clean laundry to us. With each piece I folded, I tried to lay a self-doubt to rest. What could be more calming than folding laundry? No wonder the trail was so hard for me, with its lack of simple domesticities.

I was grateful to see all my stuff laid out on the bed. Even organized in my pack, whatever I wanted seemed to have too much on top of it. "How do you manage to have what you need at hand?" I asked Porter.

"Everything has its place in my pack." He stowed each item nestled in something else—spoons and pot handle inside pot, pot inside insulating cozy, the whole kit in its nylon stuff-sack. He did the same with his first-aid and repair kits, and rolled his clean clothes inside his pack compartments.

Exhausted, we cleared our bed for sleep. Feet thumped up and down the hall outside our door, a steady stream of new arrivals signing up for showers on the bathroom clipboard. We wanted to *want* to make love, but we couldn't. We tried to inch our way toward each other across the beige sheets, but the distance seemed wider than the desert ahead.

We spent the next morning like the other hikers, sifting through and changing out gear, assembling resupplies, taking turns on the Internet, ordering pizza. But mostly we were all psyching ourselves up for the long hot stretch of the Mojave. The TV in the trailer blared that a man in a nearby town had shot his wife, five young children, and himself because he lost his job. His suicide note said he couldn't leave his kids to be raised by someone else.

My mother once told me that in desperation—two toddlers, no food, and a drunk and violent husband—she thought of turning on the gas to kill herself, my brother, and me. I was in my early twenties when she confessed this, the same age she'd been in her despair. But she hadn't gone through with it. *I loved you that much,* she seemed to be saying, *to find a way to take care of you.*

Now I waited for a turn on the phone in the trailer's kitchen to call her. Donna Saufley came and went with baskets of clean laundry. My mother and I didn't have a washing machine in our housing project. Under the weight of a duffel of dirty clothes, I would stagger a few blocks to the Laundromat, glad I had a way to help my mother.

Finally it was my turn for the phone. Every week or so when I called my mother, I wondered whether she'd be ready to have me come home to help.

But not this time. "Your brother takes me to my chemotherapy appointments," she said. "Other than that I just want to rest."

How could I explain that I wanted to take care of her, as she had taken care of me? "I've been thinking of you," I said with a lump in my throat. My words sounded stilted. "And what a great mother you are."

"Don't overdo," she said.

My mother used to keep her ironing in a wicker basket, adding to a pile she never got to the bottom of. One steamy summer day while she was at work, I dragged the basket from the closet. I set up the ironing board, high for a ten-year-old. Full of love, I ironed all day—my brothers' shirts, my mother's aprons and table-cloths—until the last piece. She hugged me when she got home.

If only it were that easy now to get to the bottom of my love—for my mother, for Porter, even myself.

A group of us borrowed the Saufleys' station wagon to drive hours to a mall outside Los Angeles to buy more water bottles and replace worn-out gear. I was rattled by the traffic, crowds, and smog, but I needed new footwear. Boots were too heavy for racing over the miles, so most PCT hikers wore running shoes that wore out quickly from the pounding.

"How long have you had those?" the clerk asked of mine, beat-up and filthy.

"Three weeks." I'd bought them back in Idyllwild.

"Three *weeks?*"

But while I tried on new shoes, Porter crawled inside sleeping bags. He bought one that was ultralight but warm down to fifteen degrees.

"A single bag?" I asked. "You really don't think I'll make it across the Mojave, into the Sierras?"

He didn't answer.

I stared out the car window on our way back to the Saufleys' from the city. I couldn't imagine leaving the trail to go back to Houston, softened as I was by the quiet of the wilderness. I struggled not to cry while the others traded trail gossip—who fell off the trail from injuries and illness, who was still on.

"Tom and Sheila took a zero day in Wrightwood because Sheila was sick," said Zigzagger, our town crier. A zero was a day with no trail mileage.

My heart sank. I was desperate to talk with Sheila. But miraculously, they had arrived at Hiker Heaven while we were shopping. While Tom unpacked their gear in the couples' room they'd been given, Sheila and I gabbed in the kitchen over Diet Cokes.

"How're you doing?" I asked. "I heard you got sick in Wrightwood."

"Yeah. But I got to watch *Oprah* in bed at the Pines Motel."

I was envious. "One of the things I miss most is *The Ellen DeGeneres Show*."

"The trail is so hard," she said, "but I'm okay, aside from red ant stings, falling down, sore feet, and rattlesnakes. Sometimes my legs feel like wooden blocks when it takes hard hiking to get to water."

"I'm a mess," I said, and then blurted it out. "Porter wants me to come off, but I can't."

She gave me her measured look. "I know what you mean. Tom wants us to hike faster and longer each day before stopping to camp. But they can't make us get off the trail if we won't go."

If we won't go.

"It's not like Porter isn't worn out too. Is Tom?"

"Oh, sure. Sometimes we think the trail is trying to kill us."

The desert radiated heat until the sun went down. Fifteen of us sat on hay bales around the campfire, drank beer, and hooted at each other's stories.

"Sheila got pollinated by a bee," Tom said.

"You're kidding," I said.

"A bee landed on my lips," Sheila said. "Brushed me with pollen before it flew on." Her lips indeed looked like a bright pink flower.

Porter pressed Donna and Jeff for why they put us all up at no charge.

"If the PCT were a marathon, people would cheer you on from the sidelines," Jeff said. "You're doing a marathon every day for months."

That morning, we had seen the truck that the Saufleys paid to deliver thousands of gallons of water a day. Besides leaving a discreet donation, what could we do to thank them for making sure we were rehydrated and showered, in freshly washed clothes?

"Someday, we may host hikers too," Porter said.

Donna eyed Porter's hiking jersey, clean but irrevocably stained with dusty grunge. "Before you go," she said, "I'd like another crack at that shirt."

The longer we got comfortable at the Saufleys', the harder it would be to leave, so early the next morning, Porter insisted we pack up.

"Can't we stay just one more day?" I asked. "Like Tom and Sheila and everyone else?"

"Not if we want to stay on schedule," he said. "If we keep up a good pace, we can make it to the Andersons' by night." Joe and Terrie Anderson offered camping in their yard, running water, and Terrie's famous taco salad.

At least he wasn't insisting I stay behind. "Later, Sheila," I hollered to her as she emerged sleepily from the trailer. I sighed, but once again, took off running after Porter.

We walked north on Agua Dulce Canyon Road, up Sierra Pelona Valley, past the outskirts of town with a few homes, a small airfield, and a church. We followed Mint Canyon Road to a dirt road, descended and ascended through chamise.

Midmorning we came to a confusing junction, where jeep and

dirt-bike tracks obscured the trail. Against my better judgment, I followed Porter up the path.

"We haven't seen any footprints," I said after an hour. "Are you sure we're on the right trail?"

"See the sun in the east? We're going north, like we should."

Didn't switchbacks lead us every which way, even if ultimately north? The path grew thick with overgrowth. "Please let's check the guidebook?" I asked.

He refused to take the time, until we stopped for water. "Okay, we're off the PCT," he admitted, "but we can still get there on this path. See where it comes out below?"

"No," I said, but I lacked the expertise to offer a better solution. Instead of learning to read the topographical maps or decode the mileage markers in the guidebooks, I'd been busy simply coping.

Porter finally halted at a brushy dead-end.

I tore the wrapper from a Snickers, chomped down hard. "We wasted three hours. Now we'll never make it to Terrie's taco salad."

We turned to retrace our steps in the midday scorch. I was furious he was wrong, and he was furious I was right.

"It was just a few miles," he said.

"More like six. Why won't men ask directions, even from a guidebook?"

"We figure it out ourselves."

"But you were *wrong*."

"It was just a little detour. You try having to be right all the time."

I flew back down the trail in a rage. I kicked myself for all the times I went along with someone else—a parent, teacher, boss, bad boyfriend, instead of my own good judgment. Little Miss People-Pleaser, pleasing everyone but myself.

I covered so many miles in my fury, Porter had a hard time keeping up. Late afternoon, I was the first to arrive at the Oasis, a small clearing where the Andersons had stashed soft drinks in ice chests, a few miles before their house. A skeleton with a PCT bandanna was propped at the entrance.

"As Daniel Boone remarked," Porter said when he tumbled in,

"'I have never been lost, but I will admit to being confused for several weeks.'"

"Daniel Boone notwithstanding," I fumed, "from now on, I'm making more decisions."

"Lord help us," he said.

Later I read what he wrote in his journal:

Oops, wrong turn but sure I can get back to trail. Oops, must turn around. Gail furious, insists on having more say.

ACROSS THE MOJAVE DESERT

FROM MEXICO: 512 MILES. TO CANADA: 2,151 MILES.
We staggered into the Andersons' home, called Casa de Luna, after dark. A dozen hikers sat outside around the picnic table littered with the remains of tacos. Terrie Anderson brought Porter and me plates heaped with fresh tortillas, beans, tomatoes, and cheese. We devoured them while the others debated the danger of mountain lions. The California population of mountain lions, also called pumas and cougars, was said to have drastically increased to at least 5,000.

"Five *thousand?*" I asked with my mouth full.

A cougar had attacked two mountain bikers not far from here that past January. One died.

"He was partly eaten, including his heart, and the rest of his carcass was buried," a bearded guy said. "Cougars cache their killed prey to protect them from scavenging wildlife and birds."

"Later that day the same lion grabbed a woman's head in its jaws, but she survived," another man said. "They attack if they're hungry."

Each male mountain lion needed about a hundred square miles to sustain himself with prey, and a female about thirty square miles. Young male lions had to stake out their own home ranges.

"We're in their space," a girl in braids said. "They're losing their habitat to forest fires and urban sprawl."

"Whatever, they got to have meat," the bearded guy said. "Deer and coyote can be in short supply on the trail, so watch out."

Others joined the debate, but none had encountered a mountain lion. Their voices rose, some strident with fear, others insistent with compassion, skeptical or full of bravado.

Porter and I excused ourselves to spread out our sleeping bag in the yard, under the moonlight.

"How do we feel about cougars?" I asked him.

"They can spring forward forty-five feet, or drop sixty feet and land running," he said. "They sprint forty miles an hour after prey."

That was so Porter, wary respect for the mountain lion's prowess and strength.

"But what if we encounter one?"

"Don't worry, we . . . "

We what? He was already asleep.

After pancakes the next morning, we left Terrie and Joe's. We hiked all day and spent a sweaty night on small, sharp rocks, being bitten by swarms of mosquitoes.

I awoke itchy and dirty. I reached for my clothes, then winced at how that hurt my injured shoulder.

Porter grabbed the guidebook to search for a road out. "We're not hiking the trail any further until you see a doctor."

"You're a doctor."

"An orthopedist. To find out what's wrong with your shoulder."

I yanked on my clothes and stuffed our sleeping bag into my pack. "I'm fine." I loaded our seven liters of water onto my pack's top and sides.

He took back five of the liters and kneeled to strap up his pack.

"If you carry all that," I said, "you'll have pain in your foot and ankle."

"I'll risk it if it helps us go faster."

What to do about this seemingly insoluble problem? "Hike your own hike" was a maxim on long trails, instead of trying to go at someone else's pace. Had we set ourselves an impossible task, or could we find some middle ground and still complete the PCT?

Could we resolve our trail dilemma as we had Porter's fundamental dilemma as a hospice doctor, and mine as a hospice doctor's wife? When we were first dating, I went to see a psychotherapist so I wouldn't screw it up. I didn't want to fall into my old pattern of advance/wrong man/retreat. But the therapist, in his deep, morose voice, said of Porter: *He helps the moribund to diiiiie.* It wasn't the encouragement I was looking for. I ran out and never went back.

Day in, day out, throughout our marriage, Porter had absorbed the pain of dying people and those who loved them. He became the steady presence that allowed for the stark reality that everyone who lived also died. I became the steady presence at home that allowed him to rest, eat, prepare to bear witness again.

No wonder he wanted to walk through the cycles of nature—death, birth, growth. No wonder I wanted to walk with him, toward nature, each other, ourselves.

I took back two liters of our water and headed in a run up the trail before he could take them away.

Help me, I cried to the emptiness of the sun-baked landscape. My heart was a rock I wanted broken open, my thoughts a tangled underbrush I wanted scorched to the ground. I ran until out of breath, out of space and time. I forgot who I was, or where, until rounding a switchback—I stopped.

Sauntering toward me was an enormous cat, tawny gold as sunlit sand. Her muscular shoulders rose and fell, her haunches swayed side to side against the solid rock of the mountainside. Her long tail flowed behind her, catching flecks of light. The world slowed to the rhythm of her movement.

Suddenly she saw me. She raised her sculpted head, looked through me with her green-gold eyes.

We contemplated each other.

Gaze, rest, gaze. Rest, listen, rest. Listen, wait, listen. Gaze, listen, be.

Finally, she didn't so much break as dissolve our gaze. She turned her massive body gracefully in the narrow space of the trail, back toward the way she came. Then she was gone.

In the absolute quiet, everything was light and clear. The mountains fell away. All there was was the loveliness of silence. I existed to listen. I was the listening.

The wind moved through the absolute stillness. I was as supple as wind, as still as the sky.

After a while, Porter rounded the switchback, straight into me. My feet rerooted in the soft dusty earth, life flashed up through my body.

"I saw—an animal," I managed.

"What kind?" he asked.

"A big cat," I said. "With a really long tail."

"How big?"

I motioned to the middle of my thigh.

He took the baskets from the bottom of his trekking poles, to turn them into spears.

"What are you doing?" I asked.

"Mountain lion," he said.

"Mountain lion?" I echoed faintly.

We continued down the trail. I hoped the lion had had enough time to move on, even as I longed for another glimpse of her. How did I know she was female? I just did. Porter went first, and I hung close behind him as instructed. We navigated between the high desert rocks on either side. Mountain lions sometimes attacked from above.

"We should make lots of noise," he said, a job he left to me.

"I'll sing." I regressed to the first song I'd learned as a child. "Take me out to the baaallgame," I sang at the top of my lungs.

Shivers ran up and down my spine as we passed between high rocks on either side. I felt her lingering presence more palpably than my own. She seemed unutterably real, where I myself seemed magically imagined.

I wasn't afraid, because I had seen her, where Porter was because he hadn't. True, she was solid muscle in her top-of-the-food-chain saunter. We wouldn't stand a chance.

"She won't attack," I said. "But what a way to go."

What a way to go. Once again the world fell deeply silent. I didn't need protecting from anything but my small, imagined self. Let that self die into love out here.

For days, from the black oak forests along the crests of the Sawmill and Liebre mountains, we caught glimpses of the Mojave Desert below. Its western edge, the Antelope Valley, stretched so wide and flat it was inconceivable we'd cross it to the Tehachapi Mountains on its other side. Thru-hikers feared it as one of the hottest waterless stretches of the Pacific Crest Trail. At the recommended two gallons a day per person, we lugged six gallons to make it the next forty miles, at temperatures well above a hundred degrees.

But when we dropped out of the mountains and struck out across the Mojave, I took to it as to no other part of the trail. The mountain lion was there, a presence within me.

All we had to do was walk. We hiked down sand-packed roads, plodded on trail as thick as beach-sand. Bees, toads, and birds were large in their purposefulness. Snakes were grand, sunning in their lassitude. How did we measure in this scheme of things? Only the intensity of our experience was big enough for where we were. The natural world was preternaturally vivid.

Our sweat evaporated instantly in the hot dry wind. Dust devils, whirling tornadoes of dirt, rose up all around us. We tied bandannas over our faces when sudden gusts stung us with sharp grains of sand.

We'd been blinded by golden dust and wind the previous year, bicycling west on our tandem from Houston to San Diego. In California's sculpted North Algodones Dunes, we pedaled for miles through a sandstorm. Thousands of centipedes rolled over and over across the road. We had skidded; the tandem fishtailed beneath us. Before we went down, I tore my shoes out of my clipless pedals, but Porter's were jammed with sand. He fell over into the road and was barely missed by an eighteen-wheeler that swerved around him. I pulled our heavy bike off him. "Are you okay?" we cried simultaneously. We were badly shaken.

Our cross-country bike trips had been hard, especially pedaling over the Appalachian Mountains on our way to Maine, and over the Rockies on our way to California, but not as hard as hiking the PCT. We had to hike ten hours a day to make our twenty miles, where we'd biked five hours a day to make our fifty miles. Most nights on our bike trips we had a chance to recover, with a bed in a budget motel, a shower, and simple restaurant food. Not to mention that the disparity in our muscle power was equalized on the tandem. I didn't have to strain to keep up with Porter, he was right there on the seat in front. Like a parade queen on a float, I loved waving at people we passed.

Nevertheless, I now found a confidence I hadn't felt before on the trail. I relaxed in this wide-open landscape, with a newfound sense of freedom, out here in the air instead of inside my thoughts, my mind.

I walked way ahead of Porter, since we could see each other for long distances. I understood that his wanting time to himself had nothing to do with getting away from me. I too wanted to be alone with the silence. Once in a while I looked far back to see whether he was still there. Even when I couldn't see him, we were still present to each other, graced with our respective solitudes in the shadeless, unlimited space.

Near lunchtime, I stopped and waited for him under the scant shade of a lone Joshua tree. Mormon pioneers named these tall, spiky-leaved yuccas after the prophet Joshua, as if pointing the way to the Great Salt Lake. With no need to talk, we ate dried apricots and cranberries, crackers and cashews. We sipped our precious water. Seemingly deserted at midday, this Joshua was home to red-tailed hawks and woodpeckers, night lizards, screech owls, and wrens. Beetles scratched in the dirt around us.

We hiked all afternoon, then camped that night in a dry sandy gully carved out by the wind.

Porter sifted through our food bags. "What'll we have? Beef jerky bourguignon? Ratatouille au rehydrated tofu?"

I eyed our bags of dried mushrooms, onions, garlic, sun-dried tomatoes, marjoram, and thyme. "Something simple." Had I been making everything—our hike, the trail, life—so much more complicated than it really was?

He cooked us plain old mac and cheese, as he did when we were caught in the freezing storm our first week on the trail. We sat close as we ate from our pot.

"Thanks for coming out here with me," he said. "We're going through so much."

"Thanks for bringing me with you." I looked into his sage-green eyes.

The sun going down in the desert was even more radiant than in the mountains. The air brightened as the sun set lower and pressed on the warmth of the sand. The desert deepened into pink, tinged with ultraviolet. The stars blinked on, glints of ice in the royal blue sky.

No sooner had I spread out our sleeping bag than a gust swooped it away. I chased it across the sand and threw myself down on it, just as Porter had when the wind blew me across the top of Mount Williamson. I laughed, less trapped inside my idea of myself.

I searched for words for the spaciousness the mountain lion had led me into on the mountainside. "It felt so familiar, so natural."

Rattlesnakes came out at night when the air cooled and the sand was still warm, down from its daytime scorch of one hundred fifty degrees. The Mojave green rattler, with its venom poisonous to the brain and spinal cord, was a real danger here. But since my experience with the lion, I felt our coexistent peace.

"Mountain lions don't reveal themselves to everyone," Porter said.

Coyotes yapped and howled across the empty space. We listened to the suck and whoosh of the wind across the sand, and felt how our bodies were made of desire, self-judgment, longing, fear of loss. My lips pressed his ear in a listening kiss.

We hadn't made love for a while, and now we did with a freedom I'd never known before. It rippled fiercely through my heart and body. As if struck with love between my shoulder blades, my body jumped, my arms flew out.

THE MISERY INDEX

The Mojave Desert was made of a sandy sediment of mountain erosion up to 5,000 feet deep. After breakfast the next morning, we set out across it again. Once in a while we saw an iguana or a collared lizard doing its tiny push-up. Green creosote bushes and low gray sage sprouted across the dusty washes. California poppies sprang up, orange-yellow blossoms with blue-green leaves.

I had learned to distinguish a rattlesnake's hiss from the wind in the chaparral. "Snake," I said and pointed to it from a safe distance. We gave it as wide a berth as the narrow trail allowed. But in the limitless outside, snakes alleviated our loneliness, or rather, shared our solitude.

Across much of the Antelope Valley, we hiked along the massive pipe of the California and Los Angeles aqueducts. Taking water from the mountains to the cities, the pipe was sometimes buried, sometimes visible—black-tarred, eight feet in diameter. Where the Pacific Crest Trail turned from north to east, the Los Angeles Aqueduct disappeared to an underground channel beneath a wide concrete slab.

We had no access to this water until we reached a lone spigot at dry Cottonwood Creek at the edge of the Mojave, two days later. Parched and grateful, we drank and refilled our bottles. Then we began our ascent into the Tehachapi Mountains.

We found one of our best campsites yet at the top of a ridge, under the branches of the largest juniper we'd ever seen. We made love again, under a sky thick with stars. Far below, whole cities sparkled in separate oases of light.

Off at 7:00 AM the next day, we dropped down from the Tehachapis through wind farms on the bare brown mountainsides. Windmills towered unimaginably high above us, their propellerlike turbines whistling eerily in the ferocious wind.

Llama, a research mathematician from South Dakota, overtook us on the trail, just before we headed into the town of Mojave to resupply. While he and Porter compared gear and the base-weights of their packs, I quizzed him for trail gossip.

"Heat, injuries, illness, dehydration … " The wind stole away his words. "Dozens of hikers behind you have dropped out."

We didn't see the cougar again, just her tracks, enormous paw prints in the sand. Five hundred and fifty miles of my own tracks had brought me here, into this limitless space. I would walk the next 2,000 miles or not. Like the lion, I would be as my nature required.

In the desert town of Mojave, we stayed in a budget motel run by an immigrant family from India. With yogic composure, the husband and father accepted our credit card. The wife and mother emerged from a beaded curtain behind the desk to give us towels to take to our room. A wide-eyed little girl clung to her mother's sari; a serious school-age boy skateboarded in the parking lot.

This motel, suspended in the stillness of the desert, evoked the Sikh ashram in the heart of Houston where I used to practice yoga. Several mornings a week, I drove from my apartment at 4:00 AM and parked between the Sikhs' vans, marked *Loving Lawns and Gardens, Nirvana Plumbing,* and *Conscious Chimney Sweeps.*

As soon as I opened the ashram door, the chants of Sadhana, the Sikhs' morning prayers, billowed out. When Sadhana was over, the Sikhs rose from their sheepskin mats and slipped out. A few other yoga students arrived.

Our teacher was a young Sikh woman, several months pregnant. She padded in barefoot, wrapped in white, her radiant face framed by her white turban. Her young daughter tiptoed by her side. They sat down together in front of the class. The teacher faced us. "Press your palms together at your heart center," she murmured.

We began with long deep breaths, then chanted the prayer to unite with our higher self. What was my higher self, and could it save me from my lower? What was my lower self? We asked for guidance in our exercises and meditations, that we might feel God flow into our bodies and minds.

We stretched and breathed our way through the poses. The tiny girl followed her mother with a childlike matter-of-factness. The names of the asanas were earthy and reassuring—frog pose, cobra, plow. At the end of class, the teacher played an enormous gong as round and gold as the rising sun. We rested on our backs with our eyes closed while the sonorous music intensified, merged with our own vibrating energies. I flew, forgot my body, drawn by the ebb and flow. The undertone of the gong was wandering and resonant, as if played not by the Sikh mother, but by the baby in her womb.

"Be sitting up," the teacher said when the last tone faded. Many of our instructions were given like this, suggesting not an action but a way of being. We sat up, brought our hands once again to our heart centers. We thanked our teacher. On the porch, we put our shoes back on and wished one another well. The trees rustled with birds.

Our Mojave motel room, with paintings of orchids and lotus blossoms on the walls, was serene and spotlessly clean. The colors—pink, lavender, and taupe—were like those in my mother's apartment. She was living, as I was hiking, on borrowed time.

"Hi, Mum," I said on the phone. "We're fine, everything's great."

"Good, dear."

"How are you?" I asked. "How are you feeling?"

"Fine, dear."

That was all. "What do you think she meant by that?" I asked Porter after I hung up. At home, after so bare an exchange with my mother, I used to call my brothers, sisters-in-law, and uncle, to ask what they thought. That was how it was in my family, you got everyone's interpretation instead of the truth from the person herself, then compared versions and fretted before settling on a composite. Each relative's take was filtered through his or her own projections, so you got a sense of how they were doing. You could then talk about that person with the others.

"We never knew what she was thinking," my uncle Warren, her brother, once told me when I asked what my mother was like as a child. "Couldn't you tell from how she behaved?" I pressed. "No," he said when he'd thought about it, "she was always reading." She read throughout my childhood too, at least when not overwhelmed by raising three children and earning a living.

"I don't know what she meant," Porter said now. "We never have to guess what my mother thinks."

We knew what his mother thought, we just didn't know why. "Is Porter depressed?" she would call to ask me when he did something she didn't understand.

"Why does she think you're depressed when you go on an outdoor adventure or spiritual retreat?" I asked him.

"She equates soul-searching with depression," he said. "Otherwise, why would anyone do it?"

"Are we depressed?"

"I'm unhappy about the collapse of my job, and anxious about the future," he said. "But no, I'm not depressed."

At Tehachapi Pass, the Pacific Crest Trail entered California's Sierra Nevada, although here it looked much like the Mojave Desert we had just crossed. Water was scarce on the brown mountains, the only shade the occasional Joshua tree. Our eyes ached from too much light. Sharp yuccas speared the sky.

We each came down with a cold and sore throat. Alternating sweats and chills, I pushed with Porter into the seventy-mile-an-hour gale. Tehachapi Pass was a wind tunnel, where the vacuum left by rising desert air filled with oceanic air, compressed between the walls of the ridges. We had been through so many kinds of wind—icy with sleet in the storm in the San Felipes, hard to stand up in on mountaintops, hot and dry in the Mojave. But these gusts roared like waves.

At Golden Oaks Spring, I collapsed and fell asleep. I awoke to find that Porter had collected and purified eight liters of water, and cooked salmon teriyaki.

"I can't eat," I rasped, "my throat is too sore."

"Mine too," Porter said. "But if we don't eat we'll get weak."

I ate slowly, carefully. I was spacey, too subdued to complain. "How do the other hikers cope with the hardships of the trail?" I asked.

"They're young athletes, with a higher misery index," Porter said. "The more they love the trail, the more misery they can put up with."

Could I raise my misery index? The deepest part of me loved the trail, it was just my body that suffered. I felt the pull of the High Sierra, snowy peaks white against the blue sky. If I lasted the next two hundred miles, at our present rate of eighteen a day, we would climb them in less than two weeks.

We packed up and walked on, uphill without traction in the sand. The trail shifted from sandy desert to swaths through meadows, forest paths to snowy glaciers above tree line, over boulders and rockslides, through creeks and rapids.

From the sunny crest that divided Caliente Creek to the west from Jawbone Canyon to the east, we descended to a blue-oak savannah. The spaciousness of the wilderness absorbed past and future into a timeless present. My old concerns faded to a hum in the background, as innocuous as bees in the bushes, the low wind scrubbing the desert floor.

I saw myself as if from a distance, as a mountain lion would from far above on the mountainside. It was intimate, as if she were blessing me. "I'd love to see the lion again," I said.

"If you see one, yell and show your teeth. Raise your arms, look big. Don't turn your back or run like prey."

I knew the drill. If attacked, fight back. Throw rocks and sticks. Don't give up. But it was myself I had been at war with for so long.

We ran out of water a couple of miles before Robin Bird Spring, only to find when we got there that four cows blocked our way. They mooed plaintively as we made our way around them and undid the barbed-wire gate to the piped water.

At the shallow spring, I knelt in the mud to wash my hair and shirt. I longed to rinse away pain like the grit in my hair, scrub the suffering from my body like the stains from my clothes. Still, the trail was working on me. Like the lion, it was a being unto itself.

We crossed the Garlock Fault, California's second longest, where it met the San Andreas Fault. It was overdue for a major earthquake. I hoped it wouldn't happen that day.

We were close to completing the length of Southern California and crossing into Central California. In my longing to elevate my misery index, I looked up through the tall pines and white firs, the black and live oaks. I spent too much time looking down at my footing, for snakes and ant mounds, loose rocks that could turn my ankle, fur and bone thrown up by long-eared owls. I became an expert at scat, stepping over cow patties and horse manure, coyote, bear, deer, and rabbit poop. Now my eyes feasted on the pink manzanita, the white-flowering phlox, and fields of purple-blue lupines. From the rubble of an old mine and a rusted bus, we climbed to a ridge crest saddle, then descended northeast, crossed dirt roads, marched up again past granite bluffs. Blue penstemons bordered the sandy trail. We found shade under golden oaks and gray-green pinyon pines.

Again, we ran out of water. I was prepared to go without, uncomplaining. At Lower Yellow Jacket Spring, we found a barely perceptible trickle of water. Porter channeled it with a leaf into his bottle.

"That's a hard way to get water," I said.

"Sometimes it's the only way," he said.

Just as each day, each hour we found ourselves in an ecosystem different from the one before, each night we camped in a different environment—out in the open on a sweep of sand, or tucked into a gully to escape the wind. Sometimes a camping spot seemed right in every regard, but had a bad vibe. We moved on until we found something more friendly. We walked around a potential site until we agreed on one. Pine needles were best, or soft sand or dirt.

We camped that windy night in a desert wash. Porter rehydrated tomatoes and cooked our beef jerky and rice.

After dinner, we examined each other's backs and legs for ticks. Ticks were common in the Southern Sierra, and I hoped our flulike symptoms weren't Lyme disease or Rocky Mountain spotted fever. While Porter caressed my bare back, I noticed the date on his open journal page—May 31st.

"Today's our engagement anniversary," I said.

Seventeen years ago this evening, he had taken me to an elegant restaurant in Houston, then after dinner to the Transco Tower Fountain at twilight. Lovers lolled in the grass. "I want to spend the rest of my life with you," he said. I hadn't seen it coming, but with the same inner knowing that had led me to hike the trail, I said yes.

"Did you have any idea when you said you'd marry me that we'd be out here doing this?" he asked now.

"None whatsoever. But I wouldn't change a thing."

"Me neither," he said.

He still carried the single sleeping bag he bought in L.A., but it stayed tightly stuffed in the bottom of his pack.

I had surpassed my earlier bumbling efforts to organize us for bed. Our foam pads inside our sleeping bag, I situated water bottles beside our respective heads. Next to my water, I placed my upside-down sunhat, and inside that, my LED flashlight, 1200 mg of ibuprofen, urinary funnel, antiseptic wipe, watch, and sunglasses to put on the next morning. I arranged my camp slippers—mere inner soles with net on top—for getting up in the middle of the night, so I wouldn't step barefooted on snakes or thorns. Next to those, I placed our folded tarp and stakes in case it rained or snowed. On my side of the sleeping bag, I lay the hot-pink stuff-sack of my clothes. I took off my clothes in a certain order, to pull them on in reverse in the chilly morning.

These simple strategies gave me no end of comfort. In this I was like my mother, making domestic order out of emotional chaos. She taught me the household arts so well that night after night, I could now make the wilderness homelike. Whatever my failings as a hiker, I knew I was a good campmate.

Just as I was learning to love Porter and even myself for who we were, with our disparate strengths and challenges, I was learning to love my mother. I was beginning to see her as simply myste-rious. In my effort to make sense of her emotional distance, I'd tried to understand her by one thing: the abuse she suffered from my father. We had experienced our love for each other as worry, mine for her during my father's reign of terror, and hers for what she considered my misguided choices.

Just as I had tried to understand my mother by the story of her marriage to my father, had I been trying to understand our hike by the story of our hardships?

Be sitting up, I heard the Sikh mother say. Simply *be.*

My mother could die while I hiked the Pacific Crest Trail. I used to believe that in her emotional distance I'd lost her long ago. But now I knew I was wrong. My heart was heavy with anticipa-tory grief. Because I wished her relieved of suffering, would I be relieved for her when she died? My love for her was quiet. I could love her now on her own dispassionate terms.

I put on the silk long johns I slept in, washed my face with an antiseptic wipe as daintily as if at a Palm Springs spa. Porter simply undressed and got into our bag. Just as he could put his hands on what we needed during the day, I could at night. If he couldn't find his flashlight in the darkness, he borrowed mine. If he couldn't find his water, he drank mine. If he wanted to know what time it was, he asked me. It didn't matter, I was probably awake and in pain.

The wind picked up. Our ultralight bag flapped fiercely, as if to take off with both of us in it. But we clung together and stayed warm.

I PROMISE NOT TO SUFFER

FROM MEXICO: 638 MILES. TO CANADA: 2,025 MILES.

We were just sixty-five miles from Kennedy Meadows, a kind of base camp before the High Sierra. While we ate breakfast, Porter cooked the hot casserole we would eat later. I loaded it in its pot on the top of my pack, which usually worked fine unless I fell down before lunch.

Porter threw himself together, but repacked his share of the community gear in a systematic way. I hoped the clear plastic pouch that sufficed as our wallet wasn't buried too deeply, on the off chance I found something to buy.

We scanned our campsite lest we leave anything behind. Lathered with sunscreen, in sunhats and sunglasses, we hefted and buckled on our packs. Trekking poles in hand, we were good to go.

Soon we were in a singed forest of pinyon pines, where a 1997 lightning fire had destroyed the brush. We scrambled to avoid the stinging poodle-dog bush that had sprung up in its place.

Three days later, Kennedy Meadows came into view on a vast field of sagebrush. The general store nestled in a grove of trees had assumed mythic significance, a goal in itself that had kept us going through our worst times on the trail.

"That's Kennedy Meadows?" I asked. Here we'd prepare for a huge transition, from the heat of the desert to the cold of the snow, from lightweight gear to heavier for survival.

A cheer went up when we clambered up the steps of the store's porch, where a dozen other thru-hikers sat surrounded by their piles of gear. The porch was the actual staging area for the next two hundred miles of Sierra wilderness.

"Have a hot dog." Jason handed each of us one off the grill.

Jason and Snake-Charmer, Wildflower and Packman, and MGD had all buzzed by us on the trail. We met Mystic, quiet and ascetic, and Weather-Carrot, named for predicting the weather, his long red hair aflame around his face. Beer-Snob was here, and Dog-Hiker hobbled about, waiting for his injured hip to heal. Each was hanging out until he deemed the snow in the High Sierra passable enough for his or her expertise. They studied the postcard Scott Williamson sent back describing the snow conditions, and waited for their ice axes and crampons to arrive.

We joined the parade of hikers darting in and out of the general store. From the store's back room, we dug out our shipped boxes of snow gear, bear canister, and food resupplies. Porter unpacked and sorted through them while I paid a dollar or two for use of the various hiker services. I waited my turn for the one washing machine, pay phone, outdoor shower stall, even for space to dry our clothes on the line with everyone else's socks and underwear. I wore my raincoat, my only outfit not in the wash.

"Stylin' rain gear," Packman teased me.

Silly as I looked in my raincoat in the broiling sun, I felt welcomed and respected for making it this far. Like Packman and his wife, Wildflower, an athletic young ecologist, pretty much everyone but me had hiked the entire Appalachian Trail and climbed mountains in Europe and the Americas. These were the extremely capable hikers the guidebooks said could attempt the High Sierra. Still, an undercurrent of anxiety electrified our joking camaraderie.

German Tourist—GT for short—kept us all hooting with her skewed efforts at English. "MGD is impregnated," she said, meaning impregnable.

I envied MGD her wiry frame, and GT her six-foot muscular one. Tall but small-boned, I felt puny and girly beside them. "How did they get that way?" I asked Porter.

"Genetics, nutrition, and training," he said.

My childhood of peanut-butter-and-marshmallow-fluff sandwiches on squishy white bread with the crusts cut off flashed before my eyes. I set about helping Porter bag dry milk and biscuit powders, protein bars and jerky. We crammed these into our metal bear canister, and when it didn't all fit, emptied it out and tried again. Since there was no hope of my being able to lug my own canister like everyone else, we had one double-sized for Porter to carry.

Our nearly three-pound bear canister, a cylinder fifteen inches long and nine inches in diameter, weighed nearly thirty when filled with food. Tightly fastened with three screws, the top was designed to thwart the smartest bear.

Porter stabilized our homemade stove for high winds, and sewed a bird feather I'd found onto my hat. We were preparing not just our gear but also our fortitude for the steep ascents in deep snow, storms on the summits, icy fords through rivers swollen with snowmelt. With no roads or even cell phone access, hiking out in an emergency would be an ordeal in itself.

Finally he took me by the shoulders and looked me in the eye. "If you're going to bail," he said, "now's the time."

But I was feeling good, for me. I'd hiked and climbed seven hundred miles. "Me Tarzan!" I said.

"Me not Jane," he said.

Regardless, I was going on. I went off to spray our clothes with insecticide, donate gear to the hiker's box, and ship ahead extra supplies.

Hikers arrived throughout the day, singly, in pairs, or small packs—Skywalker, Sprite, Goat, Sidetrack, Tigger. For the most part, they were kids in their early twenties with Herculean energy and stamina. I was glad when Tom and Sheila, our midlife compatriots, arrived.

Sheila put even her rain pants in the wash, so she hid out back in a long T-shirt while her clothes flapped on the clothesline.

"How are you doing emotionally, on the trail?" I asked.

"I can't control my feelings," she said. "They're much more on the surface than at home."

"You too? Is it because we're tired, or the trail is so intense?"

"The wind drives me nutcakes."

"I know," I said. "It's like being under attack."

We commiserated about the daily struggle for survival—weather, water, covering the miles, finding a place to make camp, then cook supper and set up the tarp for bed. From the sheer caloric output, she'd lost twenty of her extra fifty pounds. I'd lost twelve, and at five feet seven inches, was down from one hundred twenty-five to one hundred thirteen. Still, we were excited about climbing into the High Sierra.

That night we all gorged on cheeseburgers and corn-on-the-cob and shrieked at each other's stories over beer. We scooped chocolate, vanilla, and strawberry ice cream from huge tubs to make our own sundaes for dessert.

After supper, Meadow Mary drove Porter and me back to our campsite, a mile from the general store. In her sixties, she was married to Billy Goat, trail-named for his long white hair and beard. We had yet to meet him, behind us, hiking the PCT for the fourth time. Meadow Mary rode ahead in her camper to resupply him at various stops, and supported herself on donations for giving hikers short rides and massages. That night Porter treated himself and me to a massage on Mary's table under the pines. It was a luxury most other hikers couldn't afford.

"My trail-name should be 'High Maintenance,'" I told him. "Yours could be 'Good Wallet.'"

Porter couldn't relax in spite of his massage. Our gear repaired and supplies all packed, he was desperate to head out. In our sleeping bag, we had a whispered fight.

"Why not settle in for a few days, like Tom and Sheila?" I asked.

"I'm worried about tomorrow's 3,000-foot climb, and whether our food will last in the Sierras," he said. "But mostly I'm afraid you'll freak, out there."

That hurt, but he had a point. "Since the mountain lion, the trail has been working on me."

"I just love you a lot," he said. "I hate to watch you suffer."

"I promise not to suffer." I was learning that pain wasn't the same as suffering—I could hurt and still be okay.

"What if you cry and throw a fit when your life depends on self-arresting with your ice ax?" he asked.

Sliding out of control down an icy glacier, you're supposed to throw yourself on your ice ax and dig its tip into the mountain-side. "You'll teach me to self-arrest on the first deep snow we come to," I said.

"I can't get you out of every dangerous situation."

"I came out here to be with you, and now I like it too much to go home."

"I've created a monster," he said.

In the morning, we found we were out of sunscreen, but Porter refused to wait for the store to open. I went to "yogi" some from Wildflower and Packman. Porter was too proud to yogi—trail-speak for beg or borrow. But sharing made the trail feel communal, so I was glad to do it.

We left the Kennedy Meadows Campground at 6,020 feet via the Clover Meadow Trail, dipped into a side canyon of pines and junipers, and entered the South Sierra Wilderness. We marched all morning through towering ponderosas and spruces, willows and wild roses, yellow-blooming bitterbrush.

Two section-hikers racing down the mountain nearly collided with us. "Our buddy is sick," they blurted as they raced by. "We're going for help."

Soon we came upon him, a young guy collapsed in a heap. He lifted his head to give us a glazed stare, then curled up in the fetal position. He grunted thanks when Porter covered him with his jacket.

"Gastroenteritis," Porter guessed, "from bad food or water."

Unable to drink or eat, the guy wasn't strong enough to walk out. We would stay until help or another hiker arrived. We hovered nearby and let him sleep.

Sitting pensively beneath a juniper, I caught whiffs of its berries, from which gin was made. Like Proust's madeleines, they brought back the blissful part of my childhood—my mother, uncles, and grandmother drinking martinis in Grandma's backyard. My brother pinched Japanese beetles from the roses, while I read in the house, drank Cokes, and ate my way through Grandma's cookie jar.

"Having second thoughts about the Sierra?" Porter asked.

"No, just wishing I had a Coke or a martini."

"You don't drink martinis."

"I will by the time this hike's over. Are you having second thoughts about the Sierra?"

"I'm thinking about the next phase of my career," he said. "Maybe some combination of hospice and palliative care, wilderness medicine, and lightweight gear design."

Gear design?

Another hiker arrived and volunteered to stay the next shift with the sick guy. We headed up the trail, and soon after heard the rescue helicopter. Together we watched it rise above the trees.

On our 2,000-foot climb out of Death Canyon, Porter labored under his heaviest pack yet—fifty pounds, including our thirty-pound bear canister of food, both of our ice axes, two liters of water, our sleeping bag, fuel, and all his clothes. I carried twenty-five pounds—my own clothes and what I could of the community gear.

"Jeez, this is steep," he said at 9,000 feet. "But we're finally in the Sierras."

Where tree-covered mountains to the south curved like a soothing hand, to the north now rose spired peaks. We crested a ridge between rocky crags, descended through the shade of foxtail pines. From a crest-line saddle, we trudged up another seven switchbacks to nearly 11,000 feet and traversed down west-facing slopes to water from a spring in a meadow of buttercups.

Ups and downs notwithstanding, the trail led steadily higher into the mountains. The air grew thinner, our breathing more labored from the altitude. We took our descents in stride, even though lost altitude had to be regained by ever-steeper climbs. At each saddle, I stared breathlessly at the peak ahead, white against the sky.

Bicycling on our tandem from Houston to Maine, Porter taught me to gauge our progress toward the summits of the Appalachian Mountains. "We're almost to the top," he said as we pedaled, hearts beating out of our chests. "How can you tell?" I gasped. "It's getting brighter," he said. "More trees below than above, closer to the sky." I could gauge our progress myself on our second tandem trip, from Houston to San Diego over the Rockies.

But here we had no such sense, spiraling up seemingly without end. The mountain's shoulders rose higher at each round of a switchback. At 11,160 feet, California's Cottonwood Pass marked the true beginning of the High Sierra.

"What a contrast to the desert and charred forests," Porter said.

We camped at a blue lake, shallow near shore with green reedy grasses. To keep from being eaten alive by thick swarms of mosquitoes, we armored ourselves in wind pants and wind jackets, to which Porter had sewed head nets and gloves. We slipped one bite of supper at a time up through the slits in our net hoods.

I hopped and screeched, tried not to get bitten while relieving myself. All night the insects whined above our net-covered faces and buzzed with fury to get in.

Trailing clouds of mosquitoes, we set off the next morning at 7:00 AM. We hiked through forests of sequoia redwoods, ancient junipers, and foxtail and ponderosa pines. It was blissfully quiet, until we neared creeks roaring with snowmelt.

We'd negotiated mudslides and rockslides, but now struggled to keep our balance on the rocky bottoms of these overflowing streams.

"They can't mean for us to cross that," I said, when the trail led directly into deep water.

Porter didn't answer, just stepped up onto a slippery fallen tree that stretched toward the other bank. And they certainly couldn't mean for us to cross on so narrow a log.

"Let's talk about this for a minute," I said as he moved gingerly forward and frowned in concentration. I stared in disbelief.

Step by step, he inched ahead on his big feet. Halfway across, his foot slipped and he plunged into the rapids.

My scream caught in my throat. I stood like a tree rooted to the bank while he tumbled and bobbed further downstream. His shirt bloated with air and water, until I couldn't tell it from gray boulders in the white spray. I heard only the roar of roiling waves. What should I do? Bushwhack down the bank through the trees and maybe get lost? Would he want me to stay here, or go for help?

"Porter! Porterrrrr?" My holler crescendoed to a wail.

Time stopped, as it did with the mountain lion. I saw through time, to when neither of us would be here, or anywhere. No one was here, in this infinite quiet.

An eternity later, he walked up the opposite bank. He was a ghost, an apparition I barely made out.

His voice rent the silence. "Let me come get your pack," he called.

"No," I croaked. "Just wait for me there."

Too shaken to cross on the log above the deep current, I flailed through the icy water and fought for balance on the slippery rocks.

"Go back," he shouted. "Walk down the bank to where the creek is less deep."

I turned back, and bushwhacked through the brush. I walked and walked, until after a while I came to a wide but shallow crossing. The creek bottom heaved beneath my feet in a woozy, rolling motion.

"Shit, shit, shit." I scrambled up a muddy bank. Now where was the fucking trail?

On wide crossings, you couldn't see where the trail continued until you got to the other side. Wet, cold, and frightened, I stormed up the bank.

"Porter?" I cried again. "Porter. Porter. Porter!"

The forest fell silent, even the birds. It scared me to hear them listen. I was sick with the emptiness of being lost.

Finally, I heard the crack and crash of thrashing. Porter parted the branches and emerged from the forest.

"Damn it," I said when I fell into his arms. Now that I wasn't scared, I was furious with relief. "Couldn't they have put a bridge or something back there?"

"The fallen log was our bridge," he said.

"What a rotten one."

We took off our wet clothes, wrung them out, and laid them in the sun. They were still damp when we put them on again a half hour later, to continue up the trail.

Soon after, we got our first close view of Mount Whitney, the highest mountain in the contiguous United States. Thrust higher from earthquake after earthquake, its jagged gray rock speared the sky.

Although the Pacific Crest Trail didn't scale Mount Whitney, it was a side trip that few who made it this far could resist. One of the hot topics back at Kennedy Meadows had been who would or wouldn't attempt its 14,491 feet. I had no desire whatsoever to climb it. I planned to lie in the grass and take an all-day nap while Porter attempted it.

But he hobbled as we set up camp at Crabtree Meadow. "I can't believe it," he said. "I sprained my ankle falling into the rapids."

He wouldn't be able to ascend Whitney after all. He sank to the ground, went from glum to heartbroken to resigned. A herd of deer grazed in the green meadow while the sun went down.

"I've been so angry," he said at last. "At myself as other hikers sped by. Angry, just angry."

Stunned, I listened, like the deer. One after another lifted its head to look at us.

"It's not just that I wish we could go faster," he went on. "I'm angry my hospice career fizzled out. I'm furious at my parents for not seeing me for who I am, never finding me good enough. I'm mad at myself, embarrassed that I still care."

Had this been behind his long silences? How long had it been building up inside him? My feelings erupted before I knew they were there, where his came to a boil as slowly as water at high altitude.

The deer dipped their heads to nibble at the brush, and then looked up again. Listen, eat, listen. I took in Porter's words, but most of all sat with him. The evening light turned under itself, softened from orange to a copper glow.

"I forgive my parents," he said. "They did the best they could. And my teachers, bosses, mentors, everyone I looked to for approval. I forgive my ex-wife for the whole divorce drama." His voice broke. "And you're really amazing."

I amazed myself. We were both amazing. "At the bedsides of dying people," Porter once told me, "all the bullshit falls away, and they're just themselves. Even the people around them become more real." The trail sanded us down in the desert, scrubbed us with rough mountain brush, washed us raw in the rapids.

"I need to forgive—myself," he choked out. "For the pain of being a part-time dad. For getting older. I'm not hiking like a twenty-year-old, but I'm doing okay."

One by one, the deer left the meadow. They lifted their graceful necks, sniffed the air with their whole beings, then turned and loped back into the forest.

I held Porter close. We sat a long time in the gathering darkness.

THE HIGH SIERRA

FROM MEXICO: 766 MILES. TO CANADA: 1,897 MILES.
Four hundred miles long and sixty miles wide, the High Sierra
was the most remote wilderness of the Pacific Crest Trail. For our
two hundred miles close to the crest, there would be no roads
out of this alpine winter in June, no vehicles, electric wires, tele-
phone lines, cell phone access, or stores. Instead, we would hike
through a glaciated wonderland of glittering pinnacles, jeweled
lakes, and polished rock formations above the forests that made
the High Sierra the Range of Light, one of the most luminous in
the world.

Soon after Crabtree Meadows and a mile north of our ford of
Whitney Creek, the Pacific Crest Trail joined the John Muir Trail.
We hiked past solitary foxtail pines, some over 3,000 years old,
with red-brown trunks and green needle clusters. We tramped
past lodgepole pines foreshortened by avalanches and whitebarks
blown into weird shapes by the wind. Their branches clutched at
rocks, like us struggling toward timberline. Our breath came in
shorter gasps as the air thinned.

I learned new words for this strange landscape. We scrambled
hundreds of feet over and around terminal and lateral moraines—
piles of rocks left at the front and sides of glacier paths. We gaped
down into cirques, eroded bowl-shaped cliffs encircling tarns,
high green alpine lakes frozen over with aqua tints.

But it was the word "pass" that began to glow in my interior lexicon. More ominous than the "switchback" of the previous seven hundred fifty miles, a pass was our only route between thrill and fear. All of our energies would focus on climbing and descending a succession of mountains via their narrow passes: Forester, Kearsarge, Glen, Pinchot, Mather, Muir, and Selden. Each ascent and descent had its own set of terrors. But each pass opened to the top of the world, a place to stand and touch the brilliant blue sky, survey the world beneath—white snowfields plunging down shelf by shelf into mile-deep canyons and valleys.

The only creatures we saw now were pikas and marmots, found only in climates like that of the Ice Age. We heard the squeak of a pika—a small, tailless mammal—more often than we saw one. But marmots, sunning like fat woodchucks, sat high on their haunches to get a look at us. They loved a good photo-op as much as I, they posed and vogued. "Waaaait," one seemed to squeal from his rock, "I'm ready for my close-up."

The silence deepened around us, until we heard the distant roar of a waterfall. I watched snowmelt pour down the mountain and hoped for a chance to redeem myself. The trail led us through one rushing stream after another. It's just cold water, I told myself, don't freak out. I boulder-hopped across streams where rocks broke the surface. From the bank, I planned my route by the width of my stride and the weight of my pack. Once I committed to it, it was best to keep going, rather than wobble on a sharp or mossy stone. Sometimes when I got there, the space between rocks was too wide. I had to search for another or backtrack, waver while my trekking poles sought purchase in the rocky creekbed. If the rushing current grabbed the basket of my pole, or its tip got stuck in the rocks at the bottom, I plunged in and got wet to my waist, along with my gear.

We came to a creek so deep no boulders reached the surface. All that was available was a fallen log, and I was still shaken from Porter's catastrophic log-crossing a couple of days before.

"It's all about momentum," he said.

I watched in awe as he bounded onto one end, bounced a little to test its strength, then strode purposefully across. He was most magnificent the last few yards, when he ran and jumped to the bank.

I could straddle the log and scoot, but the bark would tear up my pants and inner thighs even if I managed to hang onto my pack as I pushed it ahead of me. So, pack on my back, I stepped up with shaky legs.

"What's the worst that can happen, right?" I called to Porter. "I could fall off, be carried away by the current, and drown."

"Please don't drown," he said.

You can do this, I told myself. I took a deep breath and inched across, one foot in line with the other. I kept my eyes on the log's knots and bark and watched for slippery smooth spots. I tried not to look down into the water, afraid I'd lose my balance in its flowing motion.

"You're doing great," Porter encouraged me from the other side. I felt him psychically will me across. The most frightening moment was the leap from the end of the log to the bank. By then I was exhausted from courage.

He braced one foot on the bank. "You're almost there." He reached out his hand and I grabbed it. There was a grace to it, this wilderness minuet, one we'd do over and over again. The love with which he thrust out his arm, the trust with which I took it, would become the defining gesture of our hike of the Pacific Crest Trail.

Many of the streams lacked either boulders or logs, so we had to ford them. We stopped first to take off our boots, peel off our socks to keep them dry, then put our boots back on to keep our balance and not cut our feet on the sharp, slippery rock-bottoms.

After each crossing, we paused on the other bank to pour the icy water from our boots, dry our feet, and put our socks back on. Our socks got soaked, so after each ford we alternated to the slightly drier pair, airing under straps on our packs. Some of the kids forded streams in rubbery sandals, but we couldn't carry their weight and bulk.

I had no idea we'd be fording so many streams, up to twenty a day. Twenty.

"The guidebook says Tyndall Creek is 'formidable,'" I fretted that night at our campsite.

"You're doing fine at crossing creeks," he said.

"More formidable than what we've been through?" I asked.

"We'll ford it somehow."

We had no alternative, this high in the High Sierra.

The next morning we pried open our socks, frozen and stiff as boards, and forced our cold feet into them. Our boots were frozen too. Even the laces were stiff, hard to tighten and tie with our freezing fingers.

After cold fords through Wallace and Wright creeks, we arrived at swollen Tyndall Creek. It looked even more dangerous than reputed. I held my breath as Porter crossed first to test the power and depth of the current.

"Undo your pack's hip belt," he called from the other side. "If you lose your balance in the current, shrug off your pack so its weight doesn't drag you downstream."

"And lose my pack?" I hollered back.

"Better than losing your life."

Frozen on the bank, I stared into the deep rushing water.

Finally I stepped in and lurched drunkenly even with my trekking poles. Facing upstream for balance, I slowly sidestepped across. But my foot got caught between two rocks on the uneven bottom, and the rapids knocked me down.

First there was white, the cold foam of swirling bubbles. I sputtered and gurgled, fought hard to get up, but I couldn't. I thrashed harder, and the water gave way beneath. My legs flailed above me. I sank, butt-heavy.

I landed softly on the bottom, half-reclining on my pack. I watched my sunhat rise above me to the surface. It was bright up there, but deep down here, everything was blue. I was drowning in blueness. I bounced in the upwelling, downwelling. I slipped into a blue-shift of time running backwards. I saw my mother, leaning into a troubled smile.

But someone was parting the air. He was a shadow, head to water, leaning from the sky. I looked up through web-work under water, saw the fine lace of trees, sunlight latticed through their branches. The world was halved by sunlight.

Porter plunged in and dragged me out, body, pack, and all. I sliced the air with my icy bones. We collapsed on the rocks. Water poured from us in rivulets. A waterfall of snowmelt myself, my teeth chattered like clacking pebbles.

I sat there reeling with stillness. Inside, I felt like the river, a wider, deeper version of myself. My skin tingled from the bracing cold, my eyes opened at the brightness of everything around me. Nature, much more powerful than I, let me live.

We walked on, so our feet wouldn't get frostbitten. Our body heat dried our clothes. We moved forward in the stillness, on the trail growing deeper with snow.

Snow hid the trail. I tried to read the wilderness map. Clutching it at various junctions, I turned around like a cat chasing its tail. "I can find myself on the map if I already know where I am," I said to Porter, "but what's the point of that?"

"It's good to know where you are," he said.

But I wanted to know where we were going.

"How do you suppose Tom and Sheila are faring with their GPS?" I asked.

Tom had spent weeks before the hike entering coordinates into their global positioning system, an electronic directional receiver. Even as the gearhead he was, Porter didn't want to screw around with one while trying to survive on a snowy mountain, never mind carry its weight.

"Better, I hope, than my mountain guide in British Columbia," he said. It was Porter who'd pointed out that the guide's GPS had led them to the edge of a cliff in a blinding snowstorm. "Uh, back up very slowly," the guide had said, from their fragile overhang of snow.

Instead, we relied on Porter's skill with a compass. I wore a simple plastic one on a cord around my neck, but had only the vaguest idea how to read it.

When we stopped for a rest, I puzzled over the guidebook on how to get a true reading from various declinations, like 14½ degrees east near the Mexican border to 20 degrees east in Southern Oregon. "Does my compass correct for declination?" I asked. "What is declination, anyway?"

"See that mountain peak?" he asked. "If it lies along a bearing of, say, 80 degrees, and we're hiking in this section with a 15-degree declination east, then we add them to get the mountain's true bearing of 95 degrees east. Then you find that mountain on the map, and see where you are on the trail by adding 180 degrees, getting 275 degrees, if you're using a true-bearing compass. That's all there is to it, unless you're using a reverse-bearing compass, in which case you subtract."

Whatever.

We went on, until we arrived at the foot of a high granite wall. Its polish sparkled in the morning light. We were scaling that?

"Forester Pass," Porter breathed. "It's 13,180 feet. The highest point on the entire Pacific Crest Trail."

Switchbacks blasted out of the wall of rock were completely obscured by snow. So as not to mar this pristine landscape, no signs pointed the way as they had on previous parts of the PCT. The purists who made it this high into the Sierra were opposed even to cairns, small rocks stacked to point the way.

We kicked steps into the icy slopes. Porter went first. Slowly we inched across or sometimes straight up the mountain. Gaiters around our ankles kept the snow out of our boots. We strapped our trekking poles to our packs, so we could hold our ice axes diagonally across our bodies in the self-arrest position.

"How're you doing?" Porter called back to me.

"Fine," I lied. "As long as I don't look down." The one time I did, I froze with fear at the steep plunge thousands of feet below.

Several exhausting hours later we reached the windy top of Forester Pass, and ate peanut butter sandwiches under the brilliant sun. Since my latest fall, I had stopped carrying a lunch casserole at the top of my pack. We looked far below to white snowfields and lakes strung together by sparkling rivulets. Above us, the sky was cobalt blue.

"If it weren't so windy, I could hang here all day," I said.

"I know," he said. "But check out those thunderclouds moving in."

Before we got stiff and cold, not to mention struck by lightning, we began to make our way down and plunged heel by heel into the now-soft snow. The sun's heat made the snow mushy and bowl-shaped into sun-cups. But once the afternoon started to chill, the downward slope would freeze again and make descent too dangerous. There was certainly no place to camp up here.

It was impossible to tell hard snow from soft by looking at it. We had to test it with our ice axes, then carefully with the weight of our bodies, then its slipperiness under our feet. Snow was complicated, usually soft and fluffy when it fell in the mountains in winter. But now, in spring, the sun's warmth melted the upper layers, which froze again at night. And then there was "corn" snow, layered avalanche snow, and slushy "rotten" snow.

Suddenly, descending Forester, my left leg plunged through the snow crust to my hip. I sat down hard. I struggled to get up, but my foot was stuck. I fought to extricate my leg as the ice hardened around it. Damn. It was hopeless.

"I'm stuck," I called down to Porter, who had already descended to the bottom. *Stuuck stuuck stuuuuck* echoed off the mountain.

It took him a while to labor back up. I sank deeper as the snow melted around my leg, then refroze.

Silently he dug me out enough to pull my foot from my boot, then excavated my empty boot.

Because of my lack of experience, I fell much more often than he. I got so tired of picking myself and my pack back up that I plunked down on my butt and slid down the icy slope. I steered around boulders with my outstretched legs, like a speeding human sled.

"That's a really bad idea," Porter hollered across the expanse of snow. "You'll break a leg, maybe both."

But I couldn't balance and boot-ski in a standing glissade, as he did. At the end of my slide, I stood, brushed off my frostbitten bottom, and looked back up at the swath I made in the snow. "Don't say I never blazed a trail."

Among the most dangerous hazards were snow bridges, frozen layers of snow hiding the creeks beneath. We listened for the gurgle of water, and Porter crossed first to test the snow with his weight. We could drown if we broke through to a creek too deep or swift. And our legs caught often in cavities next to rocks that radiated heat and melted the snow around them.

Just as we did on our way up to the pass, we forded stream after stream of snowmelt on the way down. We forded Bubbs Creek, then crossed it twice again, then Center Basin Creek, and still more tributaries of Bubbs. In the high desert it was switchback after switchback, now it was fording and more fording, many more before we camped that night. Our socks and boots never dried, but froze again night after night.

Thirty-five members of the Donner Party died in the High Sierra, trapped in the snow in 1846–47. The others resorted to cannibalism to survive, but I wasn't about to bite the man that fed me. Nor, I hoped, would bears. They lived all along the Pacific Crest Trail, but were a serious problem in the High Sierra, where they came after hikers' food. Their usual roots, berries, and fish were in short supply this high.

We studied potential camping sites for signs of bears—clumps of fur, carrion, claw marks, digging.

"Would a bear really want our Thai vegetables with tofu?" I asked.

"Yes," Porter says. "Not to mention our blackberry bread pudding. They're just waiting to raid the pantry while we sleep."

I stared into the dark and searched for a pair of gleaming eyes.

After supper, we knew better than to hang our stuff-sacks of food from a branch, where bears could bat them down. They sent up cubs to defeat the most ingenious rock-and-rope pulley. Instead, we repacked our bear canister with our food and everything with a scent, even toothbrushes and toothpaste.

Porter went off to wedge our canister and cooking gear between boulders, where a bear would have trouble clawing them out. I watched him disappear into the dark, far from where we'd sleep. I stared into the blackness, hardly blinking, until he emerged fifteen long minutes later.

The nights were so cold, in the teens, that we used Porter's new solo sleeping bag inside our double one. He let me keep my feet warm in the bag's limited foot space. We slept in three layers of clothes—long underwear, hiking shirts and pants, down jackets, hoods, and gloves. We set up our thin tarp as low to the ground as we could and still crawl under. We snapped our raincoats together to make a low wall, to keep out the icy gusts.

Now two months into our hike, I'd reconciled myself to the nocturnal twitching of my legs, and the pain in my thighs and torn shoulder muscle that woke me every hour. But I had developed nighttime coughing fits from the cold I caught three weeks before. I coughed myself awake, and Porter too. I wasn't unhappy, but weepy from lack of sleep and the emotional intensity of our days.

Porter unwrapped his sprained ankle to look at it.

"You hardly ever complain," I said. Just as he didn't talk of his patients' pain or the effect it had on him, and only in a roundabout way about the hospice's administrative problems. "At least not as much as I do."

"I'm not as expressive as you," he said. "I love that about you, although it tears me to pieces to see you cry. If you're not fine, I worry that it's my fault."

"It's not your fault. I feel raw, out here. I wish I could help you as much as you're helping me."

He looked at me intently. "I couldn't have done hospice work without you. It was so hard sometimes, and you were always there for me."

All I knew was to get up with him at dawn, make breakfast, send him off with a lunch so big the nurses teased him, and have dinner ready when he came home.

"One day a man, suicidal with pain, was brought into the inpatient unit," he went on. "He had cancer all over the place. We got his pain and symptoms under control, and he went home as a hospice patient. When I visited him, he was sitting in his recliner, looking out a picture window at his grandkids playing on the lawn. 'Doc,' he said and raised his glass of wine, 'this is really livin'.'"

This was really living, close calls with dying included. We surrendered to it, as if to the irresistible demands of a lover, the one the High Sierra had become. We threw ourselves with our whole bodies onto the mountains by day and nestled like hibernating animals into the high valleys at night.

We lay together, talking, listening. Our murmuring grew indistinguishable from the creaking and groaning of the tall trees above us, the soughing of the chill wind in the piney boughs.

MIND OVER MOUNTAIN, MOUNTAIN OVER MIND

FROM MEXICO: 790 MILES. TO CANADA: 1,873 MILES.

The harder I worked to be here, the more brilliantly the High Sierra shone. The air was so clear, I saw through it as I hadn't before. We were moving, not just over mountains, but through the wilderness as transitional space. From what to what, we couldn't know yet. All that mattered was to give ourselves up to what each mountain asked of us.

Even my body felt clear, insubstantial. To rise in the cold and dark, climb up and over passes in the snow, then ford countless creeks on our way down, we each needed more than 7,000 calories a day, from jerky, nuts, and dried fruit to the high-carbohydrate, high-protein casserole dinners Porter cooked. Still, my hip bones stuck out and my clothes hung off me. "I'd kill for a box of doughnuts," I said.

Going through the food in our bear canister faster than we'd imagined, we were forced to leave the John Muir Trail at Bullfrog Lakes to resupply. We hiked nine extra miles over Kearsarge Pass and down to the Onion Valley trailhead. I chatted up day hikers on their way back to their cars, until one volunteered to drive us fifteen miles into the little town of Independence.

"How do you *do* that?" Porter asked when we were dropped off at the grocery store. "I appreciate it, but I can't ask for help."

"I love to do favors for people. I guess I feel they do, too."

Early the next morning, our packs heavy with resupplies, we hitched back to the trailhead. We marched the nine miles up and over Kearsarge Pass at 11,600 feet. From the John Muir Trail where it coincided with the PCT, we began the long climb to Glen Pass, merely a notch 11,978 feet high up the steep wall. Hours later, rounding a switchback near the top, we were flabbergasted to come upon Tom and Sheila.

We hugged one another's pack-laden selves as best we could in the narrow spot. Turning from Tom to Sheila, Porter nearly knocked me off the ledge with his pack. I went from hugging Sheila to grabbing Tom, the four of us colliding like wobbling tops.

"We're like the Four Stooges," I said. Our shrieks of laughter bounced off the rocky walls.

"I summited Whitney," Tom said when we calmed down. "Sheila made it a good way before she had to turn around from altitude sickness."

"Congratulations, guys," I said. "I'm in awe."

"I'm jealous," Porter said.

"I'm exhausted," Sheila said. "I want out."

"I'm sick," Tom said. "I want meds and toilet paper."

We shared these from our resupplies, and the four of us set off to crawl along together. Sheila and I were desperate to chat, but neither of us had the breath.

Finally, we made the summit, with its view north of barren mountains against the steel-blue sky. "We killed ourselves getting here," I panted. "Let's stay here a while and recover."

"Got to get down the other side before dark," Porter said.

Sheila shot me a sympathetic look before we began a steep descent on snow and rocky brown scree. My feet slipped from beneath me on the loose stones. The guys stepped down painstakingly, where Sheila froze, bent over her trekking poles, and planned each step in dignified silence.

"What the fuck?" I shouted each time I slid, plunged, or fell. "Shit."

"Why don't you tell us how you really feel?" Porter said.

Whatever, I was sure to feel something else soon. The rapid changes in altitude from low to high then low again, in temperature cold to hot to cold and wet, in appetite hungry to queasy, and the havoc all this wreaked on my body chemistry was like being on an hourly manic-depressive cycle. Still, I was determined to continue.

Past a stark view of Dragon Peak to the southeast, we switchbacked down to ford a basin of lakes. Tom and Sheila halted to rest, but we went on. Much as we enjoyed their company, it wasn't just our different paces that kept us from staying together. We moved in our respective spheres of intimacy, the privacy of our coupled solitudes.

We descended further until the mountain spewed us out, from snow-covered rock and ice into sedges and wildflowers. In the late afternoon sunlight, California's Rae Lakes burst with willows and green moss damp with gurgling blue snowmelt.

Glowing gold, the balmy air softened my fear of crossing a submerged isthmus between lakes. Balancing on a log high over the deep water, I eased forward step by step. I clutched green-tipped branches growing from an outcrop and turned a sharp corner to leap to another log.

We sloshed on through sparkling gullies and South Fork Woods Creek between Arrowhead and Dollar lakes, past so many more lakes and streams they had no names.

Intoxicated with warmth and sun, we finally stopped to make camp in a glade. Porter read to me from the guidebook, about Paleozoic sediments and Triassic-Jurassic lava, the molten flow of time that shaped the slopes above us. The descriptions had a refrain: "metasediments, metavolcanic, metamorphosing, metamorphosed."

My freaking out on the scree notwithstanding, I too was metamorphosing. The landscape itself was changing me. I could ford creeks, climb and descend terrain I couldn't possibly two and a half months ago.

We were camped not far from a small band of younger thru-hikers, who pitched their tents together. At 6:00 AM the next morning, along came Sidetrack, named for wandering side trails.

"Don't mind me." She waved her bagel. "Just getting an early start."

We set out soon after, descending, climbing, fording. One after another of the younger people passed us—lanky Skywalker, cheerful Tigger, Mouse, and Sprite.

The kids hiking together sang to pass the time, but Porter regaled me with his vision for the future of palliative care. "We've got to start relieving pain and symptoms as soon as a disease is diagnosed, long before a person needs hospice care."

I'd explained palliative care and hospice to many a shrieking group of women at my bad-girl dinner parties. "Palliative care is like French kissing," I told them. "It may or may not lead to hospice, like kissing may or may not lead to sex." They loved taboo topics—death was up there with sex. Not that hospice was like sex. It was more like cuddling when you were too tired for futile hospital treatments.

"We need a continuum, starting with outpatient palliative care for people not too sick to get to a clinic," Porter waxed happily. "And consults for people in the hospital, followed by home-based palliative and hospice care."

I was relieved his hopes for the future were replacing his past despair. "But what about my mother, if we can't manage her dying at home?"

"If it gets too tough to handle, she can go to a hospice inpatient unit. They're great, usually with a homelike atmosphere."

We hiked by trees in various stages of growing, living, and dying. Even the dead trees nourished the soil for new growth. What would it be like when he or I was dying?

We stopped at a tree trunk that had fallen across the trail, blocking our way. He clambered over first, turned, and offered me a hand. I took it, just as I had so many times to cross a deep stream.

I made it over Forester, Kearsarge, and Glen passes, but the long climb from 8,600 to 12,130 feet over Pinchot Pass looked like it might kill me. We had to get to the top by early afternoon to begin the long descent down.

Laboring up in the thin air, I began to have chest pains, as if my lungs were bursting from the cold of snow and ice. I fought fear with resolve. My breath came in gasps, my pounding heart hurt. Just the exertion in this altitude, I told myself. What should I do? I refused to complain to Porter. If I had a heart attack, he'd know it soon enough. I took the deepest breaths I could manage and plodded higher toward the dark blue sky.

Hours later, we met a hiker plunging recklessly down. His legs bled from the rocks and sharp snow. He was a professional photographer named Rick.

"You haven't seen my camera, have you?" he asked. "I've lost it, with all my photos."

"Sorry, no," Porter said.

Rick rushed past until he was forced to turn around without finding it. Coming upon us on his way back up, he saw the tears I hid from Porter.

"Let me carry your pack," he said.

I would never make it to the top otherwise. Porter and I weren't even sure we were on the trail, buried beneath the snow. Following Rick's bloody tracks, we staggered up onto Pinchot Pass at 6:00 PM. My pack was there, but Rick was already gone. We stuffed down food and put on warmer clothes. My chest pains subsided, but exhausted from the twelve-hour climb, I fell again and again the long way down the other side.

I registered how much I had changed when I realized I didn't want to go home. This *is* home, the mountains seemed to say.

We camped at tree line at Lake Marjorie, and put up our tarp, Moonglow, to keep off the night's dew. We got up before first light, tugged on our frozen boots, broke camp, and set out. Resigned to cold, wet feet, we forded several creeks.

Tiny dark creatures, we scratched our way up the icy mountainside toward Mather Pass. Enormous thunderclouds gathered all morning.

"This is much harder than I'd imagined," Porter said. "Snowy pass after pass, day after day."

We were still scaling the last 1,000 feet to the top when the thunder and lightning began. The last stretch of Mather was the steepest; not even snow clung to the boulder-strewn trail. We scrambled for toeholds and hoisted ourselves up.

"You didn't say we'd be rock climbing," I said.

"This is called bouldering," he said.

Still, weren't we supposed to have ropes and belaying thingies, whatever they were called? And special shoes? I kept my protestations to myself.

I took the long way around boulders where my legs wouldn't stretch across gaping chasms. Like boulder-hopping across a river, I could plan my general route as long as I was willing to alter it once I saw the gaps at close range. I stopped short at a rockface too wide to see around.

Porter reached the top of the cliff before me. "Hand me your poles," he yelled down.

I stretched so he could grab the tips. Hands free, I groped my way up the rock.

"Lift me your pack," he called as I neared the top.

I did, then barely managed to pull myself over the top of Mather Pass. I flopped onto my boulder-scraped belly. "I'm good at this."

"Yes," he said. "You are."

The views of the 14,000-foot peaks of the Palisades thrilled us, until it began to rain icy sleet. Lightning flashed, thunder crashed seconds later. The storm was too close. We'd come too far to go back. We could die right here.

"Come on," Porter said. "We've got to get down the other side."

We had barely made it to the trees near upper Palisade Lake when the worst of the hailstorm struck. I ran to get water from a stream, but bruised by frozen white marbles, I raced back to throw our wet, muddy packs under the tarp Porter was frantically pitching low. He dug trenches on all sides to channel the runoff. A mix of rain, hail, and snow covered our tarp and everything around us in white ice.

I spread out our sleeping bag and pads in our low, cramped space. Porter brought water to a boil, but it took forever to cook our pasta at this altitude.

"You were calm and centered on Mather, you never lost it," he said as we ate. "You've gotten over something."

It was true. What a change from our old dynamic—me complaining, him suggesting I leave the trail.

"We keep risking our lives, but why?" I asked.

"I ask myself that a lot," he said. "But I've never felt so alive."

Life here came up close. Some wall between mountain and mind gave way, in the hidden rush of water under snow.

The last few afternoons, we hiked as far across the valleys as we could, then camped in the gathering darkness at the foot of the next day's climb. But because we'd stopped early in the storm, we had to descend the "Golden Staircase" on the cliff of the gorge the next morning. After crossing Glacier Creek, we hiked down through Deer Meadow's lodgepole forest, through the grasslands of Grouse Meadow before our ascent to Muir Pass. Once past tree line, we had ten more miles of highly exposed trail to cover before the top.

"These mountains are huge, and we're so small," I said. Even my crises, large as they seemed, shrank to nothing in the vast whiteness.

Winding up and up, we tried to follow the tracks of hikers who'd gone before us, but lost them fording stream after stream of snow-melt. We saw no one else and plunged again into solitude.

Finally we arrived at the summit at 11,955 feet. To get out of the raging wind, we ducked for a moment into the stone hut built to honor the mountaineer John Muir, legendary for his 19th-century exploration of these very mountains. Then, with no time to waste, we began our long descent, not so much steep as slow and arduous. The entire slope was pitted with sun-cups, bowls from a few inches to three feet deep hollowed out of the snow by the sun's heat. There was no sun now, just a sky blackened with storm clouds. My tears froze to my cheeks. I felt as raw as the ice-scoured landscape.

We forded Evolution Creek, fast and wide, then descended into the basin of Sapphire Lake. We camped beneath naked whitebark pines.

I was having trouble eating, despite Porter's gourmet cooking. "You finish it," I said, of the pasta with tofu left in our pot.

"Are you sure?" He devoured it. I ate less when I was anxious, and he ate more.

"Do you think I have altitude sickness? I have the symptoms—nausea, headache."

"I'm worried you're sick from drinking untreated water."

We'd run out of water purification drops two days before. We were forced to catch the cleanest water we could from mountain streams.

The next morning we scaled the canyon wall up to barren Selden Pass. We descended to Rosemarie Meadow, green and bursting with purple, pink, and yellow wildflowers. We stopped for lunch, but I still couldn't eat. Three of the younger thru-hikers hungrily eyed our peanut butter as they passed by.

"You guys need food?" I shared our extra couscous, rice, and jerky.

"Gosh, thanks," one said.

We pushed to catch the afternoon ferry to the Vermilion Valley Resort for resupply and rest. Remote as it was, hikers got there by crossing Edison Lake on a small boat.

But our fords of Bear Creek and its many tributaries were hard. We each fell in, and getting out and drying off slowed us down. It had been so long since I'd seen myself in a mirror, I wondered whether I looked as frail as I felt. I was growing so thin and weak,

Porter had to carry most of our food, water, and community gear on our long climb up and out of Bear Creek Canyon.

We missed the late afternoon ferry by just thirty minutes.

Porter stared across the water. "We could shortcut four miles around the lake to the resort. We could have a hamburger and a bed tonight."

I followed his gaze, but recalled our son Philip's description of Porter's "shortcuts" as "Dad's longcuts." I couldn't go another step, never mind wander through the forest. "We don't have a map of the route."

"How lost can we get?" he asked.

"Totally."

Dejected, he set up camp.

"We'll catch the morning ferry," I said.

"It's not just that. I'm worn out too, at the thought of going on, but I can't imagine going home."

Bucks and young does in the brush looked at us curiously. Dusk deepened into twilight, twilight into night. The stars came out one at a time.

"I have a hunger to hike the whole trail," he said. "It's been growing in me for years, intensified by work with people living their dying. But what keeps you going?"

For once, I was at a loss for words. What wanted me out here? Not my body, it was falling apart. Not my thoughts, alternately confident and doubtful. Certainly not my emotions, unreliable in their swings from high to low.

I wanted to be with Porter, yes, but even more, I felt inseparable now from the vast green and blue and white of the wilderness. I looked out on the lake, shimmering under the moon. I was as sturdy as the trees. I flowed over obstacles like water over rocks. I was as solid as the mountains, as clear as the sky.

The wind blew through my heart. I was what knew the wind. What knew the world was here in me, pulsing in trees, water, rocks, mountains, moon.

WHAT'S THE MEANING OF YOUR PILGRIMAGE?

FROM MEXICO: 877 MILES. TO CANADA: 1,786 MILES.

I awoke to the birds before dawn but went back to sleep, exhausted. I dreamed I was trying to get back to my mother's house with no way there from where I was. I lay in our sleeping bag, a *bag of sleeping*. Between sleep and wakefulness, I seemed to sense the presence of the mountain lion. Muscular and tawny against the sandy rock, she watched me with her green-gold eyes.

The stars faded from the sky. The sun came up. Spider webs broke before me as I made my way to Porter, under a pine tree on the shore of the lake. We sat in the companionable silence we'd grown grateful for. "Have a wonderful trip, and try not to kill each other," one of my friends had said before we left for the PCT. What a long way we had come since then, through differences in our skills and temperaments into this deepening trust.

Even as my body wore down, my heart opened, like the snow plant bursting red through the forest floor. Because of the mountains, the blue space of sky, the softness of green on gray rocks splashed with lichens? Or back in the desert, when colors took the place of thoughts: blue-purple lupines, creamy white yucca, prickly poppy yellow? Now, pearlescent cool air soothed my forehead and my mind settled down.

Years ago, an older lady had called our home in Houston. I couldn't make head nor tail out of what she said, except that she wanted to talk with Dr. Storey. I handed the phone to Porter. "What was that about?" I asked when he got off the phone. "She wanted to tell someone who'd listen," he said, "that she was still alive."

I was still alive, but oddly more so than before. Mist rose from the lake and I saw through it as if through myself, through light, air, flowers, trees. Beetles and ants scurried in the dirt and joined us in our silence. It seemed so long ago I believed they were out to get me, that dirt would kill me, that heat, cold, water, and ice were problems to be overcome. I'd come so far, these nearly nine hundred miles.

Sunlight glinted on the ripples of Edison Lake. We packed up and went down to the dock. Tom and Sheila, in their safari outfits, sat leaning against their packs.

"We tiptoed by you in your sleeping bag hours ago," Sheila said.

I smiled, but had nothing to say.

Thru-hikers Buzz and Izzy were there too, in their matching leather sunhats. We hadn't seen this wiry couple since our first few weeks on the trail. The laugh lines in Buzz's face were etched more deeply from the sun. Izzy was small-boned like me, but her arm and leg muscles had acquired more definition, where mine had all but disappeared in my thinness.

The ferry, a small motorboat, pulled up and we all hopped in. Tom and Sheila sat in the stern, Buzz and Izzy faced us where we sat in the prow, our backs to the spray. The wind blew back Izzy's long blond hair as we sped across the lake.

At the shore of Central California's Vermilion Valley Resort, we jumped from the boat into the water with our packs and trekking poles. Run on a generator, the resort was actually a hunting and fishing camp for visitors who drove up the rutted mountain road in their trucks and SUVs. The camp was littered with tents among RVs and cabins, Dumpsters and trash piles, with a four-room motel next to a combined store/office/café. An underground pipe had burst, and a roaring backhoe tore back and forth into the earth.

"What we have here is a situation," Porter said.

The camp was undergoing a change of management. "Just like me," I joked wearily. But thru-hikers were grateful for this outpost, and the staff, who loved hikers, welcomed us warmly.

"Listen up," the store clerk said. "Pick up your resupplies in the back. See me about laundry and stuff."

We retrieved the box we'd had shipped there, then weighed ourselves on an ancient scale on the store's porch. Since weighing in at one hundred thirteen pounds two weeks before, at Kennedy Meadows before the High Sierra, I'd lost another ten pounds.

"How could I have lost twenty-two pounds since we started the PCT?" I asked Porter. In just a few months, I went from one hundred twenty-five to one hundred three. True, we'd climbed and descended 27,000 feet in the last two weeks, nearly the equivalent of ascending Mount Everest from sea level. No wonder I felt weak and my clothes hung off me.

"I've lost only nine," he said. "That's with stuffing myself, while you hardly ate. And we're not out of the High Sierra yet."

"I've got to stay here a while to eat and sleep," I said. The conventional wisdom of thru-hikers, if one can call anything about them conventional, is that you shouldn't quit the trail without resting a few days first. "Maybe you should go on, and I'll meet you later up the trail?"

Astonished, Porter studied me. We walked at my slow pace to the communal cabin we'd been assigned. Inside, we threw our packs on bunk beds covered with bare mattresses.

"This won't work for me," I said, as the primitive cabin filled with boisterous hikers and their gear.

I went back to the store to see whether we could rent one of the vacant private trailers for the night.

On the store's porch, I met a gnome in long white hair and beard.

"Billy Goat?" The legendary wise old man of the trail, hiking the PCT for the fourth time?

"I am," he said.

I felt I'd climbed the highest peak in the world and been granted an audience with its reclusive sage. "Billy Goat," I asked, heart pounding, "why do you hike the trail?"

Billy Goat searched my eyes. "When someone asks me that, they're usually wonderin' it for themselves."

I wobbled into the store, then back to Porter, the key to a private trailer in my hand. We moved our stuff into it, then I barely managed my usual chores of laundry and rinsing out water bottles while he repaired our gear and repackaged our food resupplies.

We spent the evening in the camp café, catching up with Tom and Sheila. Still, I had little to say.

Porter and I went back to our trailer. He held me, and we made vulnerable, tender love.

"How can I bear to leave you," I asked, "if I leave the trail?"

He stroked strands of hair from my face. "If you need me to, I'll leave too."

He loved me that much? Did I love him enough to let him go on without me?

The next morning I awoke spacey and tearful, paper thin, wafting like a leaf in the wind.

"I thought I'd feel better once we got here, but I feel like dirt."

"I know. You usually bounce back at a resupply stop."

Was this one of those junctures where the thru-hike is about mental rather than physical stamina? But my drive hadn't failed me, it had gotten me further up the trail than I had dreamed possible. "You're so determined," a former boyfriend used to scold me when I kept my own counsel. Like Porter, I followed through on projects when their success seemed most in doubt.

"I want to keep going," I said, "but my body just won't do it."

"We could stay here another day or so and see," he said. "If you feel better, we could go on thirty miles to Reds Meadow."

"Is there a way out from there?" I asked.

"Another eight-mile walk to Mammoth Lakes, then we'd figure it out."

"I can't imagine hiking even to Reds Meadow."

Porter himself was at a loss, his shoulders slumped, arms hanging by his sides. Now that I had reached my actual limits, he didn't want me to leave any more than I did.

He went back to sorting and cleaning our gear, and I went to find Sheila. What little time we'd had together had been so real, I could tell her anything. We sat together on a fallen log. She put her arm around me while I cried.

"I feel awful." It was hard to get the words out. "I'm thinking of going off the trail."

"Tom's sick too," she said after a while. "His gut problems keep coming back."

"Would you two want to share a ride out," I asked, "if I can find one?"

She motioned Tom over, explained.

"I'm not quitting," he said. "They'd have to helicopter me off the mountain."

He didn't look great, but not nearly as gaunt and pale as I did.

I walked back to our trailer, and reminded Porter of the day-hiker airlifted out. "I won't put us through that," I said, "even as the drama-queen I am."

"What does your inner knowing tell you?" he asked.

"It says to come off the trail."

To my surprise, his face fell. I thought he would be relieved. He would miss me as much as I him.

"Whether just for now or for good," I said, "I want to recover at home."

"Let's see what wants to happen," he said.

That was our way of seeing what fell into place. I went to talk with a VVR staff member about finding a ride out.

My longing to continue died hard. I agonized while Porter and I struggled to reorganize and repack our food and gear for any one of three scenarios: my leaving the trail that day, or in a few days, or staying on.

"If you go, take home Blueberry and leave me Helium," he said of our sleeping bags. It was as sad as deciding child custody. "I'll send home Moonglow as soon as you send me Starshine," he said of our tarps, "and once I'm out of the Sierra you can send me four-ounce Spruce-Limb."

I stared at the huge pile of gear he'd need to go on alone—stove, fuel, water filter, satellite phone, first-aid kit, ice ax, poles, not to mention clothes, food, and water. "How can you possibly carry all that?"

He sighed. "Same as everyone else, I guess."

Within an hour, the VVR manager had found me a ride to the Fresno airport. "They're pretty much leaving right away," she said.

"Right now?"

Porter and I frantically divided the rest of our gear. I couldn't think, my mind was blank. I just stuffed into my pack whatever Porter handed me to take home.

The van drove up. Porter held me while I cried.

"I love you, Gail."

"I love you too, Porter." We had been inseparable 24/7 for nearly three months, and now we barely had time to say goodbye.

The kind couple drove me hours in their silver SUV to the Fresno airport. I caught an evening flight and landed in Los Angeles close to midnight. LAX swarmed with weary travelers. Numb, I took the first hotel van I got a seat on. I was baffled to find myself unable to sleep on a pillow-top mattress in a luxury hotel.

Later I read in Porter's journal that he left the Vermilion Valley Resort on the afternoon ferry, and spent that night alone below Silver Pass. His journal reads:

After Gail left, I cried and cried, then struggled to make four fords and six miles before dinner. Now I'm in a swarm of mosquitoes, in this gorgeous Sierra, so heartsick I can't finish my supper. Lord, please watch over us while we're apart. Reunite us soon.

Wobbly from weakness and lack of sleep, I was back at the Los Angeles airport by 5:45 AM to check in for my 7:45 AM flight, but the line to get through security was several hours long. Moving so suddenly from the deep solitude of the wilderness into this mass of people made the airport feel surreal, wavy with phantom shapes and forms.

"I should have spent the night in this line," I said to the man behind me, who didn't answer.

My 7:45 AM flight left without me.

Like a wounded animal, I wanted only to crawl back into the wilderness. My heart broke with longing for Porter and the mountains.

"Who *are* you?" Porter used to ask in our early days together. "Who are *you?*" I would ask. The loveliness of the question wove its way so deeply into our life together on the trail, we no longer needed to ask it. We couldn't even know our answer, we could only be it.

Who am I? reverberated through me now, all around, through the airport public address system. The airport was full of us, our eyes meeting in this question. In our collective awareness of even the question, I moved from fear to an odd peace.

I hung around LAX with my backpack for a midafternoon flight. It was delayed, and later I floated around the El Paso airport for my connecting flight, also delayed. From the trail, my body had spit me out, into this, right here, wordlessly full and strangely peaceful now.

UP, EAT, WALK

AFTER TWO DAYS OF HARD TRAVEL, I landed as softly as a tuft of cottonwood seed in our loft on the east side of downtown Houston. While Porter slept beneath trees on the Pacific Crest Trail, our friends Kellye and Fritz had picked me up at midnight at the Houston airport and seen me safely home. Colleen and Doug had filled the refrigerator with food. Trail angels, all.

The Houston dawn was smoky orange, tinged with rose. I awoke in the bed made for Porter and me when we married, of wood carved from a single tree. I was held in the memory of its branches.

Sun threw light on the yellow walls of our loft as if onto a mountain ledge. Everything was just as we'd left it. The concrete floor, stained earthy red-brown, was cool on the soles of my feet. I marveled at everything: the shower's cascade of hot water, the kitchen light, the gas stove where I boiled water for tea. Through the glass east wall, I watched clouds glide in the blue above flat warehouse roofs. After living outside for three months, I eased into this airy space. I didn't have to pack up and rush down the trail, didn't have to go anywhere at all.

Three months of mail collected by Colleen overflowed a plastic bin. I opened a thick envelope on top. Our former neighbors had sent pictures of our old house bulldozed by the developer who bought it. I studied the photos of collapsed rooms we had remodeled and lovingly decorated, and the garden we had land-scaped, all reduced to a pile of rubble. It was exactly how I felt.

Still, I was a steward of this body, nearly transparent with thin-ness. I made a doctor's appointment, and found I didn't have a bug like Giardia or Cryptosporidium from drinking untreated water. I was simply exhausted and malnourished. With rest, my torn shoulder muscle would heal on its own.

I slept long hours and tried to eat. At first I managed just cereal for breakfast, a salad for lunch, a veggie burger for dinner. Gradually I added calorie-laden snacks—milkshakes, chocolate chip cookies.

Downstairs in the lobby, I poured a cup of coffee and helped myself to a complimentary muffin. I had loved this building the moment I walked in, nearly a year ago. "Free muffins in the lobby," I said to Porter. "Most expensive free muffins we'll ever eat," he said as we signed our lease.

Perky leasing agents in stiletto heels clicked across the floors. Most of the residents were young and worked downtown in corporate offices, bars, and restaurants. We smiled at one another as they crossed the lobby on their way to the cybercafé and gym. I rested in deep anonymity here, free as a wraith in this sleekly sensual ambience of modernist blond wood and metallic curves, aubergine sofas beneath bright abstract art.

At a loss with myself, I felt soft with others. Everyday kind-nesses came easily—helping a neighbor carry groceries from her car to her apartment, righting an overturned plant in the hallway, kneeling down to speak with a child. Like sun warming cold mountain air, fierce tenderness pervaded the air we breathed.

Each afternoon I trekked down to the loft mailboxes and hoped for some word from Porter. To save the battery on his satellite phone, we'd agreed that I would read the journal pages he sent home a few at a time.

One afternoon, after I had been home for a week, I met the postal carrier sorting the building's mail.

"Thank you," I said, when she handed me mine.

"What?"

"You're doing a wonderful job."

"All people do is complain," she said. "Where's their mail in all this junk, no one by that name at this address."

"I'm sorry," I said.

"I'm no better, complaining," she said. "But my back hurts, I hurt all over."

Impulsively, I gave her a hug.

Upstairs, I tore open the dusty envelope of green waterproof sheets sprawled with Porter's handwriting. His vowels were open, his capitals strong and well formed, all as well proportioned and forthright as he. His journal pages described the rhythm of his days:

Up, eat, walk, walk, up, up, down, down, ford, up, up, eat, down, down, eat, up, down, sleep.

Without me to talk and commiserate with, he wrote to himself, with his guileless mix of ecstatic vitality and despondent pragmatism. Food was so important on the trail; he wrote as passionately about that as about his deepest feelings. As long as I'd known him, he'd felt deeply about food.

June 21/ Reds Meadow, mile 901

Pushed hard—24 miles to beat restaurant closing and black rain cloud. Restaurant had one 'dinner special'—tacos, otherwise burger or sandwich. I ate a turkey sandwich and shake, then another sandwich and shake.

He bought fruit from a man who wanted to know why he was hiking the trail for six months. "You learning a lot about yourself?" the man asked. Porter wrote:

What am I learning about myself?

— Most of the time I have stamina, skill, and good sense.

— I love nature in all her moods, the stillness, quiet.

— People, especially my family and friends, matter to me.

— *We have a very short time here, we'll fade away like the flowers.*

— *I'm part of the cycles of life, and they're ultimately beautiful.*

I loved the simplicity of his insights. I felt his pleasure at views of Silver Pass in the sun, volcanic towers and domes, junipers and flowers, the night sky. Without me, he covered miles at his own speed of twenty to twenty-four a day. He kept pace now with younger hikers: Sow, Red Baron, and Prig, Juniper, Priest, and Prophet, Buzz and Izzy, Sisu and Raru, Wicked and Disco, Dude, Chinaman, and Iceman.

While he walked north the next couple of weeks, I did a lot of stopping and staring into space. I let the impact of my nine hundred miles on the trail settle into me. My journey was now an interior one, but should I be doing something? If so, what?

A wave of compulsion shuddered through me at all that needed to be done: handling mail, laundry, and household tasks. But a gift of my deep exhaustion was that I couldn't afford my old drivenness. On the trail, I took care of each task as it presented itself. I could do that—just the next thing.

Up, eat, walk.

I missed hiking. I put on my backpack and hiked two miles to the supermarket. I shopped for what I now knew Porter needed for resupplies—jerky, salsa, dehydrated tofu, beans, rice, pasta, Snickers, and Toblerone chocolate. Even heavy with groceries on the hike home, the pack felt good on my back. While Porter climbed mountains, walked through forests, and forded streams, I negotiated construction zones and waded through traffic. In my sunhat and hiking shorts, I wove among office workers marching in and out of downtown skyscrapers. The eyes of homeless people met mine.

Back in our loft, I spread the groceries I would ship to Porter on the dining room table for sorting and rebagging. With love and longing, I repacked our resupply boxes for just him instead of the two of us. Over the next couple of months, I'd lug them one at a time to the post office or UPS store, depending on what a particular outpost required.

Porter's journal read:

Got confused where two trails split. But beautiful sound of flowing water. I feel so broken open. I just want to walk and walk. Listening, opening.

Should I forcibly reclaim my old driven self, or just rest in life's stark grace?

I thought of my mother, the afternoon sun slanting through her window, lighting up her hair like sun through a cloud. Relieved that I was back in Houston, she still followed Porter on her map of the Pacific Crest Trail, and I kept her posted on where he was. "He's been through Tuolumne Meadows and camped in Yosemite National Park. He's happy, doing fine."

Her breast cancer seemingly in remission, she was as taciturn as ever. But since hiking the trail, I could be with her in her silence. Silence was textured, even full. What kind of silence was hers—anxious, peaceful, shy? Would I sense it if I listened deeply enough?

I loved her as she was. I saw her quietude as softness now, instead of distance. She was as much a mystery to me as she'd always been. But initiated into mystery—by my strange peace at not completing the trail, by the unfathomable love within and around us, I loved mystery itself. It drew me close to Mother Earth, my mother, Nature, my own nature.

Bears wanted Porter's food; deer ate his socks for the salt. He hung his shoes from a tree limb each night, but a marmot stole his watch for the salt in its wristband, from beside his head while he slept.

June 24/Matterhorn Canyon, mile 956

Fell on a wet rock crossing Virginia Creek and rolled in pack first, head downstream. Clothes drenched, ugh. Then slipped on a snow patch and landed on my back, hard. The fine carbon fiber rod I use as a pack frame is broken. Crap—now what? Lost my remaining trekking pole when it flew over a waterfall.

Porter being Porter, he splinted his frame rod with a tent-stake. Without his trekking poles, he fell in rain and sleet. The soles of his shoes lost their edge for gripping ice above hundred-foot drop-offs. He reached the 1,000-mile mark in a pensive mood:

Thought about Super Tramp's response to why he was out here— "It's a privilege. So few people can physically, financially, psychologically manage this." Grateful and happy in spite of dangers and pain.

I called Porter's mother often and reassured her as I reassured myself. Could it be that our difficulties with her, or anyone, arose from our troubles with ourselves? Weren't we all as vulnerable as marmots shivering in the snow, the desert cracking with dryness, trees groaning with wind?

I had no face to present to the world. I missed our guileless hiker friends—Tom and Sheila, Zigzagger, MGD, Dog-Hiker, Jason and Snake-Charmer—who hadn't looked in a mirror for so long, they had dropped their faces, too.

"Don't think of coming home as a defeat," our Houston friends reassured me.

How could I explain I was in love with failure? I'd thought I would find myself on the trail, but failure had brought me here to the fullness of what was left, beyond body, mind, persona.

I sat in the loft complex park, a small patch of nature reclaimed from the city's asphalt, with young green trees and pink crape myrtles. You're a sapling like us, they seemed to say. People walked their pets among the trees. In the clear eyes of the dogs, I saw the love we shared with Odin, the chocolate Labrador retriever we rescued on the trail. A cat looked down from a loft window, with the imperturbable gaze of the mountain lion in the high desert.

Evening descended on the city, and I climbed the stairs to our loft. The Maxwell House factory sign—a huge neon coffee cup—blinked on. Steam rose from the chimney and the rich smell of coffee rolled in like fog. While Porter sat by a stream at dusk, I watched the streets flow with red and white car lights. He listened to birds settle down for the night. I heard people in nearby lofts. The young couple next door came home and turned on their music, loud with a thumping beat. "And I'm like, duh," she chirped. He rumbled back in his low bass, their talk trailing off into lovemaking murmurs.

Beneath my physical exhaustion and emotional debris, I felt a curious excitement.

I missed Porter, but even his coming home wouldn't help me. We needed our respective solitudes now. I cherished this vibrant stillness.

PORTER-AND-GAIL

FROM MEXICO: 1,093 MILES. TO CANADA: 1,570 MILES.
While I recovered at home, Porter got sick on the trail. He called
me from the emergency room of a South Lake Tahoe hospital.

"Bad water, or food poisoning from a town restaurant," he
moaned. "I was already miles down the trail when it hit me in the
middle of the night—gut cramps, diarrhea, dizziness, nausea, the
works."

"Come home, right now," I said.

"I crawled out of the woods," he went on, "and called a taxi from
my satellite phone. I thought I'd die out there of dehydration."

"A taxi?" I would have laughed if I hadn't been so freaked.

"I'm okay," he said.

Soon back on the PCT, he filtered his water in addition to purifying it with drops. But the difficulties of the hike were catching
up with him. Without me there to voice doubts, he was forced to
face his own.

July 4/Desolation Wilderness, Central California, mile 1,109

*I'm weak and dizzy, thousands of mosquitoes whirling around
me in the scoured-out basin of Desolation Valley. The gray snags of
dead trees rise like ghosts from the shallow lakes. If I ever think of
doing something like this again, remember: too long, too hard, too
much pain, miss Gail.*

I kept this page by the phone to talk with him about it. I rehearsed how I'd comfort him if he too decided to come home. But by the time he called a few days later, he was past his doubts.

"Sierra City, California, mile 1,197," he said. "Last night I slid down a creek bank and got pretty wet, but I slept great and got off at 5:00 AM. It's gorgeous—rolling green hills and rushing waterfalls."

I clutched his tear-stained journal page. "But in your journal, you wanted off the trail."

"Nah, I'm just blown open—awed and humbled, heartsick and homesick at the same time. I can do the miles, and my gear is honed down and working. I'm here with Chinaman, Sisu and Raru, and Leather Feet. They're fast, but I'm steady. We're all learning from each other, trading war stories of the hike. This afternoon was rough with rocky uphill trail, but I'm learning just to be with what is."

I shopped for replacements for his worn-out gear. He wore out his shoes every four hundred fifty miles, so I bought two more pairs of New Balance 1100 shoes in 13EE.

The store clerk laughed at me. "These are not gonna fit you."

I just smiled.

I bought replacement cartridges for his water filter, nut butters, and blister pads. I unpacked boxes of gear he shipped home, washed clothes and reshelved them in our gear bins. I scrounged through the bins for items he needed—liner socks, insoles, a warm jacket, insect repellent.

Tree cover and clouds overhead made it hard to get reception on his satellite phone, so when he did, he got right to the point. "Every time I call, I ask you to do or get something," he said.

"It's my job," I joked.

He'd hiked out of the High Sierra, its snowy mountains red with alpenglow. "I had a 5,000-foot climb out of Belden. Now I'm in burned and clear-cut woods."

He crossed from Central to Northern California and reached the halfway mark on the Pacific Crest Trail at mile 1,331. He sent me a birthday card handmade on his waterproof journal paper, signed with greetings from Sasquatch and Leather Feet, One Gallon and Fritz, LaundroMat, No Way, Siesta, and Steady. I read the note scrawled by a woman who drove Porter into town from a remote trailhead: *From one support person to another. Happy Birthday, from Spirit, the thru-driver.*

Deer nibbled Porter's clothes at night. He hiked close behind a fawn who couldn't find an exit from the trail. The forest was overgrown with poison ivy and hot with no breeze. He camped on a ridge, and wrote in his journal:

I crossed a bridge over a dry lava creek bed. I'm leaving my old life behind. All new over here. After passing over—strong, peaceful, free. Effort, feeling, beauty, but no 'self' in the middle, I'm dissolving into just here now. What a long, strange trip this is.

What a long, strange trip this was for us both. While I walked up and down the stairs to our loft, he walked over ridges with views of Mount Shasta, Castle Crags, Marble Mountain. I sipped wine by the loft pool with friends; he filtered water while a 300-pound bear drank downstream. Ants crawled across his face as he tried to sleep, hooting owls woke him early morning. Cows plodded before him on the trail for miles. I wove through crowds on the streets of Houston and beamed at people smiling back.

Climbing 4,000 feet of hot switchbacks, Porter ran out of water. At the top, he found only a trickle guarded by yellow jackets and a rattlesnake. "I was scared, reaching through the swarm," he told me later on the phone. "The snake was there for mice, and flashed its tongue but didn't bite."

His ordeals were as intense as ours were in the High Sierra, but in more rapid succession now that he was hiking faster.

"I'm keeping up with Richard, who was a sergeant major in the Green Berets," he went on. "He'd dive onto a remote island, rescue fellow soldiers, and swim back out into a black ocean."

"But is he looking out for you?" I asked.

"We don't hike together, necessarily, but we look out for each other. At Butcherknife Creek my feet hurt so badly I had to stop. He got worried and hiked back to find me."

Older than most other thru-hikers, Richard and Porter shared a mutual respect. The younger guys weren't so much every-man-for-himself as dominant males who clashed like young bucks.

"At 6:00 PM in the Marble Mountain Wilderness, I wanted to push on to Paradise Lake, but Richard convinced me we'd gone far enough," he said. "We talked about 'enough'—money, possessions, power. What a freeing insight."

"You've come a long way since your Sears Roebuck catalog," I said. Porter's mother used to sit him down as a little boy and make him find something to want. He would do chores to earn money, and he had been driven ever since.

Now, while he repaired his frayed pack with fishing line, I sold or gave away extra clothes, furniture, and household items that dragged me down with too-muchness. I agonized before buying the new computer I needed for my writing. The screen of my old computer had inexplicably turned pink—words, icons, everything, and nothing I tried would turn it back. I configured a new computer, learned new software, and checked email. While Porter marched up steep trails with views of Kangaroo Mountain, Siskiyou, and the gash of Green Pass east of Red Butte, I checked his email too—invitations to speak, requests for journal articles, and job notices.

By the end of July, Porter was still forty miles from the border of California into Oregon. At mile 1,656, he had more than 1,000 to go.

"I'm between volcanic mountains, north of Mount Lassen, approaching Mount Shasta," he said on his next phone call. "But the closer I get to the end of the trail, the more I worry about finding a new job."

"Job offers are pouring in," I said. "When you get home, I'll tell you which one you've accepted and where to report for work."

He laughed. I laughed too, but it seemed now that everything would happen as it should.

"Actually, the American Academy of Hospice and Palliative Medicine is looking for an executive vice president," I said.

"That's my dream job," he said.

The deadline to apply for it would come and go while Porter was still on the trail, so I updated his curriculum vitae and requested letters of recommendation for him. I left messages on his satellite phone and got back to his colleagues with his responses. He had to make a quick turnaround at his resupply stops, so I prioritized and got phone numbers for people he would call himself. He wrote his mission statement for the job on a piece of Tyvek torn from his groundcloth, and mailed it to me to type up and send.

He crossed the border from California into Oregon on August 2nd, at PCT mile 1,698. The next day, on a pay phone outside a Safeway supermarket in Ashland, he interviewed for the AAHPM job with the president-elect of the board.

"How'd it go?" I asked when he called me right after.

"Time will tell," he said.

But he wouldn't be back in time to proof a new edition of his *Primer of Palliative Care,* so I printed out the revisions, pored over the PCT route, and express-mailed them to him. He painstakingly edited them on the front steps of various wilderness post offices.

"I would have missed all these deadlines if you weren't there," he said.

"I would have missed the Pacific Crest Trail if you hadn't taken me with you," I said.

"Oregon's cool and green. I wish you were here with me now."

We were on such parallel journeys, our respective locations hardly mattered. "I feel I'm on your hike with you."

"*Our* hike," he said. "Our trail-name is now officially 'Porter-and-Gail.'"

We were working in sync, as we had on the trail. Physically apart, we were together in a new way, and we gave ourselves up to it.

A lizard jumped from a box of worn-out gear Porter had sent home. It ran across our bed and under the pillows. If it slipped between the mattress and the headboard, I'd never find it. How would I sleep? How had I slept in the woods surrounded by so much wildlife?

I got our "bug-catcher," a cup and a piece of cardboard we used to capture transgressive critters. We never killed insects—flies, mosquitoes, June bugs; we transported them outside where they could thrive. "Is this how God feels about us?" we joked when we let them go, frightened but alive.

But lizards were the hardest to catch. Their speed called for a steady hand, gentle enough not to lop off the tail. This one emerged from the pillows, stared up at me from the bedspread. Could I put aside my squeamishness and convey calm instead of fear?

In one smooth motion, I brought the clear cup over him and slid the cardboard beneath. Together we walked down the stairs. Out on a patch of grass, I released him to the wider world.

HEART MAIL

After six weeks at home, I longed to go back to the trail. Thanks to the wonders of chocolate, I was regaining the pounds I lost in the High Sierra. I worked with a trainer in the loft complex gym, but I wasn't strong enough to jump back on at the speed Porter hiked now. My hiking with him our first few months had slowed him down, and now he was in danger of not finishing before the snow in Northern Washington unless he kept up his twenty-five-mile days.

I hatched a plan to which he agreed to help him resupply quickly through part of Oregon. I would drive to a succession of trailheads and hike in to meet him. We would hike back out to the car to drive to dinner and a motel. The next morning I'd drop him off at the same trailhead and meet him again a day or two north.

I flew to Portland, rented a car, and drove five hours to Shelter Cove, a rustic resort on Odell Lake in Oregon. I paced outside our cabin and looked toward the direction from which Porter would come. Hours later, I recognized him from so far off it was as if with my whole being. He walked out of the woods in the same graying jersey, patched khaki pants, and broad-brimmed sunhat he wore when I last saw him. He looked thinner but still strong, striding toward me with his pack on his back. His even more scraggly beard couldn't hide the grin on his face. I inhaled his musky smell and wiped my teary cheeks on his shirt, worn but washed in the water of mountain streams.

A chipmunk dashed around the kitchen while I cooked our supper of rigatoni with tomato and basil, spinach salad. We sipped red wine with our dinner, on the porch overlooking the cove.

"I saw ospreys with fish in their talons, a bobcat, and meteors over Summit Lake," Porter told me. "I was eye-to-eye with a cub who scrambled up a tree. The mother bear came after me, so I ran."

I told him about the postal carrier at our loft, and the love I felt for even strangers now. About the lizard that jumped from the box he sent home, what a triumph it was to be still enough to capture and release him.

After dinner, we slipped into the cabin's bottom bunk to make love. An enormous butterfly stared at us from the top bunk's underside. I shrieked when it came after us. Porter thrashed wildly when it flew into his ear, as if to tell us something.

We stared at each other. A butterfly. Our Butterfly Route.

Over the next twelve days, I dropped off Porter at one Oregon trailhead, and met him a day or two later at the next trailhead with a road crossing. Randy, Porter's best friend and best man at our wedding, and his wife, Martha, gave me the use of their cabin on the McKenzie River while Porter covered miles on the trail.

Porter and I met near Forest Road 5897, then Elk Lake, McKenzie Pass, and Santiam Highway. I hiked in several miles with my pack, water, food, my own sleeping bag and tarp, in case we didn't meet and I had to sleep out alone. My pack felt great on my back. I was thrilled to walk again in the woods. Hiking in to meet Porter was the first time I had hiked alone.

It was vital I not get lost. The first day I hiked in to meet him, I got so confused I turned around after a half mile to go back and reread a sign. Where was this trail headed, in case I never got there? "Bobby Lake 8½ miles," it said. But where the heck was Bobby Lake, and was I supposed to head for it?

I studied the guidebook: "Bobby Lake Trail 3663," it said, and "Moore Creek Trail 40 to Bobby Lake." The "trail to" and the lake itself didn't always mean the same thing. There was only one well trodden trail—wasn't that the PCT? Then I came to another trail crossing mine, no signs, just three branches pointing off the trail. PCT hikers clarified crossings this way for the hikers behind them, but sometimes it was just a signal to a friend where to camp.

I sat down on a rock and tried to calm my pounding heart. If I were truly off the trail, I wouldn't meet up with Porter. Who or what was out here? Absorbed in such fears, absorbed in myself and my body and feelings, I had missed so much of the wilderness in my nine hundred miles on the trail. I didn't want to do that anymore. *Nothing was missed,* spoke a silence deeper than my thoughts. *No one is lost.*

Gray light shone through the silhouettes of the trees. I followed their leafy greenness down their textured, rust-red trunks. Their shadows approached along the dark brown earth to where I sat. *I'm here. Here I am.*

I realized I was on the trail after all. I went on.

After a while a hiker walked toward me.

"Are you Richard?" He looked like the Green Beret Porter had described.

"Yes," he said, startled.

"I'm Porter's wife." I threw my arms around him in a grateful hug.

"Where's Porter?" he asked.

"A few hours behind you, I hope. I'm hiking in to meet him."

He grinned and loped on. Just as Porter had said, Richard was on a schedule of the miles he would make that day.

I ran into the northbounders I had met before I left the trail— Wildflower and Packman, Sisu and Raru, Paparazzi. They were astonished to see me. We sat on boulders to eat lunch and catch up.

"We heard you were off the trail," Wildflower said.

"I'm just back for my conjugal rights," I said.

They got a huge kick out of that. After lunch I resumed my hike toward Porter hiking toward me.

One evening, I picked him up at the trailhead on Highway 242 at McKenzie Pass, and the next morning drove back to drop him off. We hiked in several miles together and left the Oregon forest of tall Douglas firs for miles of volcanic rock, post-Pleistocene outpourings of lava up to 3,000 years old. Hot and treeless with no signs of life, these lava moonscapes were slow going but deep with quiet.

"Damn, I've lost the basket and tip of my trekking pole," he said.

I found it lodged in the broken rocks when I hiked back out myself.

I logged almost 2,000 miles in Oregon, driving the rental car through towns named Sublimity and Sweet Home, past the Highway 20 Church of Christ, the Pick-A-Part Auto Wreckers, and a wooden shack signed "Drive-Through Espresso." A trail angel now myself, I drove Too Obtuse and Quixote a couple of hundred miles to Eugene.

Porter and I ate in rustic restaurants crammed with chain-saw art—large wooden sculptures of bears. We drove together several miles over a boulder-strewn road in pouring rain, to drop off his resupply box at remote Olallie Lake Resort. We were forced to back up slowly for half a mile to make way for a pickup driving out on the muddy cliff side.

On August 23rd, the morning I was to leave to go back to Houston, Porter called the American Academy of Hospice and Palliative Medicine from a pay phone outside a rural café.

"They officially offered me the job of executive vice president," he said when he came back into the restaurant.

"And?" I held my breath.

He smiled broadly. "I'll start October 1st."

Love all over my face, I studied him while he devoured his omelet.

"What's the matter?" he asked.

"I'm just making a heart print." It was our term for memorizing love, imprinting this moment indelibly on our hearts.

We made deep heart prints of each other, paid our bill, and left. I dropped him off in a gray drizzle at the trailhead at Santiam Pass.

"It's an accomplishment to live out in the rain." He walked away into the woods.

On the trail , there was no "inside" to go to except one's own.

He headed into a three-day downpour that dumped seven inches of rain. A hiker drowned fording a swollen creek. Clouds blocked reception on Porter's satellite phone, so back in our loft in Houston, I didn't know whether he was alive or dead. He wrote in his journal:

August 25. Shook up from the ford of Russell Creek, a deep, milky torrent, I missed a crucial turn and pressed on at least four miles, wet, cold, lost. That night I built a protective wall of rocks, logs, and bark on the windward side, and crawled in.

But the next morning, it was still pouring. Although he'd picked a spot with drainage, he woke up in a sea. He put on his sopping clothes and packed up his wet gear to hike sixteen miles to Olallie Lake. The trail ran deep with water. His feet numb, he waded ford after ford. Climbing higher and higher, he walked sideways in the fierce wind. His hands burned with frostbite, his twisted knee ached with every step. If he fell and got hurt, he might not survive.

I knew none of this until I read it in his journal later.

At a ridge crest at 7,000 feet, the trail disappeared into a snow-patch. All footprints gone. No signs, and fog cut the visibility to ten feet. At Breitenbush Lake, a maze of trails, I sat down to eat and look at the map. I'd taken another wrong turn. My teeth chattering, I wolfed down some nuts, but told myself can't sit long—getting too cold too fast, MOVE.

Olallie Lake was nearly deserted when he got there; the vaca-tioners had cancelled because of the rains. Porter's icy hands could hardly hold a pen to sign for a tiny cabin, never mind split wood for its stove.

Back in Houston, I grew frantic with worry, unable to get through to Porter's satellite phone or the cabins at Olallie Lake. I stared out our loft windows at the thunderstorm moving in. White clouds blackened with silver tint, heat lightning shot through the green air. Flash floods filled the streets and underpasses and brought traffic to a standstill. Sheets of rain lashed at our windows. The loft ceiling leaked and splashed giant drops on the floor.

I worked on Porter's next resupply box, and put in dinosaur-shaped pasta, truffle-infused olive oil. "No more peanut butter," he had said, "for the rest of my life." I bundled jerky and ramen noodles, sour cream powder and nutmeg, dried mushrooms and minced onion, with a small bottle of red wine for a quick beef stroganoff. I imagined him sinking exhausted at the end of the day against his "cooking rock," grateful to just add water to heat wasabi noodles, ginger sauce, and dehydrated shrimp. I planted lipstick kisses on his granola bars, tied love-notes on the rice, and stuck small neon decals of footprints on his next set of guidebook pages.

At night, I dreamed of the ceiling falling in, water cascading down the walls. I fled through a trap door beneath, but the house rocked on waves. Terror seeped through the walls of my mind.

Porter's nights were restless too:

Last night the mice went wild. They chewed up my pot cozy, dragged off plastic bags I needed, ate holes in my socks, ran over my legs and head. I put my bug netting over my hat, to keep them off my face.

In the Mount Hood Wilderness of Oregon, he hiked through new terrain—an underbrush of huckleberry, rhododendron, goose-berry, and corn lily, shaded by hemlocks and lodgepole pines. He forded creeks thick with volcanic sediment and scaled slopes to glacial cirques.

He called when he finally got reception on his phone, despite more rain, sleet, and snow. I was weak with relief just hearing his voice.

"The first day and night of rain, I can keep dry," he said. "By the second, things are damp. By the third, my gear and I are wet through."

On September 1st, he walked alone out of Oregon and into Washington, on the Bridge of the Gods. "No sidewalk, no shoulder, just open metal grate with the dark Columbia River 1,000 feet below."

On the ridge top of Table Mountain he put up his tarp to camp, but the wind was so strong he took it down, packed up, and hiked in the dark to find a tucked-in spot. "A branch crashed a few yards away," he told me, "probably a bear."

From then on, our phone connections grew even more tenuous. The battery on his satellite phone warped, grew loose, and cut us off. We were disconnected four times in one two-minute call.

"Where are you?" I asked the moment I heard his voice.

"Around mile 2,200, I think. Near a pond."

That's all I knew to tell rescuers if I never heard from him again.

My mind went crazy with catastrophic scenarios. I read the latest pages from his journal, of gunshots around him in the forest. Had he been shot by a hunter? Was he sick, or had he fallen in a ravine and broken a leg? Had he been knocked unconscious or mauled by a bear?

The closer he got to the end of the PCT, the fewer people he saw. It was too cold and rainy for section hikers. Nearly all the thru-hikers behind him had bailed, or flip-flopped ahead to Canada. To flip-flop is to get a ride north to the finishing point of the PCT and start hiking south to beat the worst weather. If he got lost, he could be out there a long time before anyone found him, and no one would if he were off the path.

I stared at the map on which I'd highlighted the Pacific Crest Trail. From the west end of the Bridge of the Gods at an elevation of 180 feet—one of the lowest points on the PCT—he had to climb to nearly 7,000 feet through damp forests, lava flows, glaciated canyons, and high alpine landscapes. One stretch circled an active volcano, another was exposed on the narrow ledge of a vertical cliff.

I reminded myself of his capabilities. His courage got him both into trouble and out of it. If he got lost barging ahead without consulting the map, he could find his way back. His sore feet had taught him to be content with hiking a steady twenty miles a day instead of twenty-five. "I stayed up half the night watching *The War of 1812* on the History Channel," he said when he finally called me from a motel at a resupply stop.

"You never watch TV," I said.

"I know," he said. "But I related to the struggle."

I was going through it with him, from a distance that mattered less and less.

I tore open each envelope as it arrived with the latest pages from his journal:

Past cliffs, spires, waterfalls, Mount Adams. St. Helens, Rainier. Scared shitless today when I got lost, out here alone with animals, weather, gear problems. Goat Rocks Wilderness, Snoqualmie Pass. The important thing is not when I'm going home, but that I am home. Who's returning, and to where?

We sent each other heart mail, messages through our hearts. One night, I awoke and bolted upright when I heard his voice, as loudly and clearly as if he were there with me.

"I love you so much," he said.

"'IP THE 'AP"

MY MOTHER HAD PROMISED not to die while I hiked the Pacific Crest Trail, at a family dinner on my visit to her before we left.

"Okay," I'd said, "but when you're dying, be sure you let me know."

"Why?" she asked.

"I want to be with you," I said. "I'll be good at it."

My two brothers and sisters-in-law had looked at me, horrified. It wasn't just that I was married to a hospice doctor and wanted to understand the dying process myself. I longed to share so intimate a moment with my mother, to somehow find a closeness we had lost, or maybe never had.

I had learned so much from the natural world about the deep silence of love. If my mother—silent about so many things—let me be with her when she died, might that mean she'd come to trust the woman I was now?

I didn't want to take a chance on her dying with no one beside her. My father had died alone. He fell asleep at the wheel on Cape Cod's Route 6, drove into oncoming traffic, and was broadsided by an SUV. "He had three terminal illnesses," Porter said of my father's heart disease and two types of cancer, "but it took a Hummer to get him off the planet."

True to her promise, my mother hadn't died while I was on the trail. But the cancer seemingly in remission had come back, now in her lungs and bones.

"Don't worry," a hospital doctor told me over the phone, "as soon as the antibiotics take care of her pneumonia, we'll do further treatments for her breast cancer."

"I'll be on the next flight," I told my mother.

"Wait and see," she said. "I may need you more later."

But the next day, she sounded worse. I pressed the receiver to my ear to hear her hoarse whisper and decipher what she wanted from me. She could say "wait and see" until her last breath.

My brother, Mark, picked me up at the airport. I was struck by the contrast, even more than usual, between Houston's perpetual greenness and Boston's crisp shift into its red-brown fall.

"I'm so worried about Mum," Mark said.

We talked and comforted one another. He recounted the time as a three-year-old he had asked me why so many bad things happened to us. I didn't know how to explain, at ten, our father's drunken violence, our mother's fear. "Bad things happen in every family," I said.

At the hospital, I was stunned to see how much my mother looked like her mother had. Instead of my mother's thin face and short hair, Grandma's wave of gray swept back from my mother's brow, her face puffy from fluid buildup, her eyes paler blue than before.

"Mum." I kissed her.

A drop slid from the corner of her eye, down her cheek. "I'm glad you're here, dear."

I cried while she slept. Washing the tears from my face, I stared into the mirror as if into the river of time. I looked like my mother used to, just as she now looked like hers, the female head of the family visibly passing from one generation to the next.

I held her swollen hand, let it rest in mine. She stretched hers from time to time to relieve the pain in her arm from the IVs. Her breathing was labored, exhausted.

"I'm so sick," she murmured through her oxygen mask.

I wished she were on hospice care, but she suffered from the same misconception so many others did, that hospice meant "giving up," instead of after a life well lived, letting go.

What could I say? I was at a loss. "You're being brave."

"'Ip the 'ap," she gasped.

"What?" I leaned closer, but she was too exhausted to repeat it.

I puzzled over it, then smiled to myself. "Skip the crap," she'd said. Still my mother after all, no tolerance for sentiment.

She grew worse as the day wore on. I slipped from her room to call my brother Dave, out of state. "You might want to come," I said.

"It's that dire?"

All along, our mother had worried that Dave hadn't come to terms with her dying. I had worried she was dying for quite some time. Mark was somewhere in between.

"Yes," I said.

I went back to her room, where her IV beeped for refills of one drip after another—antibiotics, potassium, sodium chloride. Time and again, I pressed the call button for the nurse.

"Everything takes so long," my mother moaned.

"Can I turn off the beeping while we wait for you?" I asked the technician.

"Don't touch a thing." She scowled, then bit her lip.

I sat by my mother's bed, hour after hour. All I knew to do was watch, wait, be with her.

She opened her eyes. "I'm miserable."

"I know. What can I do to help?"

She could hardly breathe now. Her air-loss mattress, to prevent bedsores, heaved and rolled beneath her.

I tried calling Porter again and again until I finally reached him in the wilderness on his satellite phone.

"I'll find a way off the trail, right now," he said.

"No, you're in your last week, and my mother could go on indefinitely like this. Finish and fly home from Vancouver."

"Ask her doctors for a small amount of morphine for relief of her shortness of breath," he said.

"They're afraid of respiratory failure. What happens to the people who have no one to go to bat for them?"

"They spend their last days, even weeks, in unnecessary misery."

"I'm so glad I came," I said. "I've felt nothing but love since the moment I entered her womb."

"Womb?"

"Room, I mean."

I wished my mother had a hospice doctor like Porter, but she would have to make do with me. Armed with her medical directives and durable power of attorney for health care, I began a hospital campaign for her comfort. Far from causing respiratory failure, a little morphine let her relax. Invasive surgeries unlikely to help were postponed and eventually cancelled. Less desperate with pain, she could talk with me.

"Gail," she said.

"I'm here, Mum."

"Water?"

I slipped a bent straw past her oxygen mask. My fingertips felt the cool liquid rise to her parched lips.

The hospital settled down for the night, except for the steady stream of nurses and technicians who came to check her vital signs and change her IV bags. But they were all busy with other patients when my mother's hearing aid wailed. She fought to sit up and swing her legs out of bed.

"What's the matter, Mum?" I stared into her wild eyes.

"Fire alarm."

"It's your hearing aid." I took it out, but unable to shut it off, ran and left it whistling at the empty nurses station.

When I got back, she was still struggling to get out of bed.

"You can't, Mum," I said.

She stared over my shoulder. "Someone's at the door."

I turned around. No one was there. Porter had said this sometimes happened when a person was close to death. Finally she lay back resigned, as if waiting for someone to come for her.

I curled up at the bottom of her bed. I reached up and held her hand, to feel the life still in it. I slept one fitful hour at a time.

Dawn brought a change of shift. The day nurse was a new mother on her first day back after five months of maternity leave. "Sorry, I'm all thumbs," she said as she changed the IV.

I was all gratitude. She and the others were simply doing what they'd been trained to do, and they were kind to my mother and me.

"Go for your walk," a nurse's aide said. She hummed a hymn while she cleaned the room.

When I came back, the room felt suffused with love, draperies open to the sun and red-orange trees outside. Ambulances came and went on the circular drive below. My mother had been lifted and straightened in bed, her head arranged more comfortably on the pillow. But she wore a startled look when she opened her eyes.

"Everything's okay," I said. "We'll all be okay."

She didn't speak.

"I love you, Mum," I told her.

"I love you, too," she mouthed.

We sat there together. She raised her hand weakly to her brow. I massaged her forehead lightly, and thought I saw her smile, a slight upturn in the corners of her mouth and eyes.

Her doctor came by, and we talked while she slept. "She's about as peaceful as I've seen." He had stopped pressing for further treatments, agreed to more morphine at regular intervals instead of just each breathing crisis. "Does your brother out of state understand he may not get here in time?"

"Yes," I said.

"Some people have the memory of the person as they were, full of life," he said. "Others, like you, of her final days and dying."

I was so grateful to be here. What if I were still on the trail? Porter once told me that a dying person often seemed to choose who was there when they died. Some hung on until a loved one traveled halfway around the world to their bedside. Others, surrounded by family, waited until everyone left the room.

My mother drifted in and out of sleep. Time moved irregularly, jumped from noon to 3:00 PM, then dragged from 3:00 to 3:07 PM. I tried to guess what she needed. The oxygen mask rode up her face and pinched the inside corners of her eyelids. I lifted it and saw a flicker of relief. I replaced it gently, a little lower. I loosened the elastic mask straps digging into her cheeks, fleshy from IV fluids.

"I'm right here, Mum, if you need anything," I said, unsure whether she heard me.

A wave of panic rolled over me. I ached with the loneliness of my love for her. How should I prepare for the coming night, the following day, night, day? I'd learned from Porter and his work with hospice that the main thing was simply to be present. It was right that Porter stayed on the trail, right that I was here.

I grew roots into the floor. I wouldn't leave; she wouldn't die alone. Suddenly I knew: this was why I had hiked the trail. Here were the cycles of nature, sapling into tree into snag. Spring melting snow into valleys purple with wildflowers. The Mojave green rattlesnake molting on the sun-baked summer desert, fat brown bears foraging for berries in fall's flaming bushes. Snow falling on high mountains, dawn spreading crimson into morning, evening gliding into night.

From my mother's west-facing windows, I watched the sun set behind the trees, a burning disc that blackened the leaves. I grounded myself in my own body, centered myself in an unnamable presence filling the room.

Mark and his wife came by. He was the closest to our mother; he'd visited her nearly every day for years. They played Scrabble and joked. Too upset to watch her dying now, he left soon after, he and Carol wordless and in tears.

"You'll need to take care of yourself, to be able to care for her," Porter had told me, just as he'd told countless others. Visit after visit for years, I practiced yoga in my mother's kitchen, and now it seemed the most natural thing to do by her bedside. From mountain pose to tree pose, I flowed from one yoga asana to another, standing poses for balance, backbends for energy, seated forward bends for calmness. Then I meditated. When I finally opened my eyes, I closed the curtains. It was dark.

The hospital settled down. I sat, my chair half in the darkness of my mother's room, half in the light of the hallway. From time to time I got up to search her face for signs of distress. Her eyes began to glaze over, unseeing when she looked at me. I looked more deeply, for light—for life—in her eyes.

At 9:30 PM, I wanted to lie at her feet as I had the night before, but there wasn't room, now that she lay extended in the bed. I made myself small, wedged in between her and the bed rails.

Exhausted, I fell in and out of sleep. The staff was not to disturb her, but at the 11:00 PM shift change, a new aide came in to take her blood pressure.

"She's Comfort Measures Only," I said. "The chart says not to check vital signs.'"

The aide was indignant. "Do they know you're staying the night?"

"Absolutely." I had no idea whether they did or not. In any case, I wasn't budging.

I moved in and out of waking. Was I awake or dreaming when the bed rail seemed to grow into a wall of flowers—unnatural red, deep blue? A young girl with bobbed hair, like my mother as a child, sat on the ground in this garden. She was waiting for she knew not what. A hand reached out to her. She rose to take this hand, and left.

I awoke from this half-dream as aghast at its picture-postcard sentiment as my mother would be. But whose dream was it? I felt like an observer of her dream. I studied the outline of the blanket over the curve of her abdomen—did it still rise and fall? Or was it just the movement of my own breath, rising and falling?

Somehow, I sensed that she was gone. She didn't look different and her cheek was still warm. The noisy rush of air from the oxygen made it impossible to tell whether she was breathing or not, and it saddened me that I couldn't know. I lay down beside her again.

I wanted to protect her from an overzealous aide rushing in to resuscitate her. "Stay and make sure," Porter had said.

I stayed and bore witness. I did a loving-kindness meditation for my mother: "May you be peaceful. May you be happy. May you be free from suffering and danger."

At 3:00 AM, the night-shift nurse came in for the scheduled morphine injection.

"I'm not sure she's still with us," I managed.

Startled, the nurse looked at her more closely and checked her pulse and heartbeat. She turned to me. "I'm sorry," she said.

Now that this moment, approaching for days, a year, a lifetime, had come, I didn't know what to do next.

"I'm sorry," the nurse said again. "I'll send in the doctor."

She left, and a few minutes later a young doctor in scrubs came in. Suspended in a strange curiosity, I hovered by the window while he examined my mother. He'd tell me something I already knew, and yet I wouldn't be surprised if he said she was fine.

"Your mother has passed away," he said.

Why was it so hard to take in? What did it mean, she passed away? I had passed through the luminous space between peaks of the High Sierra—Kearsarge Pass, Pinchot, Mather and Muir. Where was the pass between life and death?

As soon as the doctor was gone, I nestled again beside my mother. She felt like a sun-warmed boulder at the end of the day.

MY EMERGENCY DIME

MY MOTHER ONCE GAVE me an emergency dime. I was ten that sweltering day we moved to the housing project. She had to go to work, and I was to wait in our new apartment for the moving van. I was panic-stricken with responsibilities I didn't know how to fulfill. How to speak to the moving men when I was afraid of men, starting with my father, from whose violence we were escaping. Where the furniture should go, in our echoing apartment on an asphalt landscape where I knew no one. How to take care of my two younger brothers, running off to the dump that served as the project's playground.

It must have been as hard for my mother to leave me there as it was for me to be left. "Here's a dime," she said, and hugged me. "If you really need to, find a pay phone and call me."

I grew that day from merely shy to deeply anxious. I kept the dime—that particular dime—with me at all times when my mother and I were apart. If I had no pocket, I hid it in my shoe. Later I kept it in the pocket of my school uniform, and throughout my adolescence in my small red leather purse. I didn't use the dime, for fear there would be a bigger emergency when I'd need it even more. What became of it?

Now, walking alone into my mother's apartment, I felt her physical absence. Why wasn't she there at her favorite end of the sofa, her feet on her suede hassock, book in her hand? I listened in vain for her muffled footfalls on the carpet. Bewildered, I walked from room to room, their soft pinks, turquoise, beige.

On her kitchen counter, a piecrust mix sat next to lemon filling. But next to those, Tums, a piercing sign of her nausea. I was more saddened by her suffering than by her death. She'd been so private, so reserved, it had been hard to know how she felt. I attuned myself from early childhood to a sadness that deepened the more I sought her. It became the way I knew my love for her.

I called my brother Mark to tell him she had died.

Next, I called my brother Dave in New Jersey. "Mum knew you were coming. She loved, loves you."

I unpacked the plastic bag of her things, labeled "Patient's Belongings," given to me at the hospital. In her closet, I hung her blue robe and nightgown. I put her cosmetics purse, with her glasses, comb, and hearing aid, on her dresser. It was what she would do, if she were here. But she wasn't.

What should I do with everything else—get-well cards, and the last crossword puzzle she'd done, half-finished in pencil so faint I could barely read it? I studied the puzzle, as if I might discern some message in the shaky letters: "ajar," "sirens," "woe," "unity."

A thousand decisions would need to be made. But right now, I was exhausted. I unfolded the convertible sofa bed in the den my mother had used as her guest room. It was where I always slept when I visited, but now I felt I was opening my own tomb. Was it still my place, in the privacy of her space?

Hanging in the window were the turquoise agate wind chimes I had sent her from the trail for Mother's Day.

I found sheets in her closet and made the bed.

Numb with grief, I fell into a dreamless sleep.

Porter's phone call awakened me later that afternoon. Still half-asleep, I listened while he told me a forty-five-mile section of the PCT was completely closed to both hikers and stock because of flooding and mudslides. Seven crucial trail bridges had been destroyed, and the trail was impassable. Even the detour had high fords and was steep and hard to follow.

"A hiker who attempted the detour got lost and died of exposure," he said.

Disoriented from waking up in my mother's apartment, I didn't know what to say.

"How's your mother doing?" he asked.

"She died." It was the third time I had said it that day, but instead of giving reality to my mother's death, the words made me feel less real.

"I'm so sorry. Are you okay?"

"I'll be here several days. Best to call me here."

"I'll try," he said. "It won't stop raining, and the reception's bad."

"Where are you?"

"Trap Lake, in the Cascades. The dark lakes are so deep, Gail, and the mountains high through the mist. A forest ranger stopped to tell me to take a paved road around the floods and mudslides."

"So that's what you'll do, right?"

A long silence. "That's what the other hikers are doing. But my feet are in such bad shape they can't take the pavement."

He tried to change the subject by asking the details of my mother's death. But now that she was gone, I couldn't think past keeping him alive.

"Hold on, I'm calling Jan," I interrupted. My matron of honor at our wedding, Jan lived with her husband, Bill, in Seattle. They were expert hikers, they knew the Pacific Crest Trail. With Porter still on my cell phone, I reached Jan from my mother's phone. Within a couple of minutes, Jan had promised to pick up Porter and drive him around the most dangerous part of the detour.

"Jan will pick you up tomorrow afternoon in the parking area off Highway 2 at Stevens Pass," I told Porter. "Can you make it there by then?"

I heard the crackle of his voice and could only hope he heard me. The phone disconnected, he was gone.

My brother Mark, his wife, Carol, and I went to dinner at my mother's favorite Chinese restaurant. Together, we allowed ourselves to miss her more than we had alone. They leaned in to listen to my account of her last few hours.

"She seemed surprised, but ready," I said.

She would be proud of how capably we talked over the arrangements. It was Tuesday, and we agreed to have her memorial service on Saturday. We divided up the tasks. Carol would order the flowers. I would write her obituary, as well as a eulogy to read at the service. Dave would be here by then, and act as a sort of M.C. In the meantime, Mark and I would choose a container our mother would approve of for her cremains. These would be placed in the plot with her parents.

For the next two days I was consumed by small tasks. I washed the sheets on my mother's bed, cleaned out the refrigerator, and wrote notes to her friends. I canceled subscriptions and paid bills.

My mother had pared down her life, so one task followed simply after another. "People die the way they lived," Porter once said of his hospice patients, and my mother died organized.

Jan drove hours to pick up Porter at Stevens Pass, and took him back to their home for warmth, food, and recovery. Two days later, Jan and Bill took him to a trailhead off Highway 20 at Rainy Pass. A blizzard was coming down hard as he disappeared into the mountains.

"Porter was the most grateful houseguest we've ever had," Jan told me over the phone. "He was so happy we had a roof."

"I can't thank you enough." She and I had been best friends long before I met him, then during our turbulent courtship. A drama-queen even then, I subjected her to my "he loves me, loves me not" roller-coaster ups and downs. "Don't I look like a doctor's wife?" I asked, in my black boa and fuchsia leopard leggings at my bachelorette party. She'd watched me cross over to love in all its potential and terror.

"I can't believe you hiked nine hundred miles," she said.

"Porter has already hiked 2,600."

"That's just Porter being Porter," she said. "I'm glad you were with your mother when she died."

I was glad my mother lived to see me happily married. How relieved she must have been to see all three of her kids settled, after her struggles to raise us. At my wedding reception, on the patio of an elegant Houston restaurant, she patted my hand. "You've come a long way from the project, dear," she said. I laughed and hugged her. "Yes," I said, "haven't we all."

I had brought PCT guidebooks with me to Boston, since I didn't know how long I'd be here. Now, my mother gone, I studied them, as if I could psychically help Porter negotiate the dangers. Jeffrey P. Schaffer and Andy Selters' *The Pacific Crest Trail, Volume 2: Oregon & Washington* said: "Problems: Very early and very late season hikers should be ready for treacherous snow slopes, avalanche hazards, and dangerously exposed hiking along parts of this PCT section."

How late was "very late"? Ice and snowstorms on the high summits were already driving thru-hikers off the glaciers of the North Cascades. If Porter didn't get lost, would he be okay? What did "dangerously exposed hiking" mean? Ledges and precarious ridge tops? Long open stretches with no tree cover?

Finally he called from his satellite phone. "It snowed all day," he said. He had tramped high to a ridge top in icy wind and had to watch his footing along the steep drops.

"How deep is it?" I asked.

Clouds interfered with the reception and we were disconnected.

"A foot where I plunged down for a drier campsite," he said when he got through again.

"But the trail's still passable?" Disconnected again.

"It's cold," he said on his next try. "If it gets to several feet—"

"Where are you?" I demanded.

Click.

I willed the phone to ring.

"Almost to Glacier Pass," he said. "If you don't hear from me in—"
Shit.

I studied my copy of Benedict "Gentle Ben" Go's *Pacific Crest Trail Data Book,* then noted the date and time Porter called next to Mile 2,614. Forty-nine miles from the end. Two and a half days at his twenty-mile pace, plus a day and a half to be slowed down or lost. *"If haven't heard from Porter in four days,"* I wrote a note to myself, *"call Ranger."*

I sorted and organized what of my mother's to keep, what to give away. She had asked that each of us take back the gifts we'd given her, but I wanted her granddaughters to have the lapis necklace and the silver bracelet. I rummaged through her jewelry box until I found a ring she wore in my childhood. When I was seven, I printed *I love you* on a tiny piece of paper and stuffed it into this ring, a hollow silver globe on a simple band. This I would keep, along with her butterfly pin, small ivory wings outlined in gold. It fascinated me then, and fascinated me now. It seemed a symbol of our envisioned Butterfly Route, the overlay in the shape of a butterfly on a map of the United States, biking the inner wings, hiking the outer wings.

On Thursday, Dave arrived. He and his wife and two grown daughters chose what they wanted to remember my mother by—framed prints and china. Mark and Carol chose books and a lighted ceramic Christmas tree. After they left, I waited for a moving van to come and take the remainder to a women's shelter. Just as I'd waited for the moving van to come, so many years ago. I no longer needed an emergency dime.

My mother's apartment nearly empty, all I had left to do was wait. Wait for my mother's memorial service, and wait for Porter's call. But there was no word from him. He was almost through; why was I so frightened now? I relived our conversation; it was the fear in his voice.

I read the names of the passes in the guidebook—Cutthroat, Windy, Foggy.

I looked at it from every angle. He wouldn't take stupid chances. He was experienced in snow. He had enough food and water. But the part of the trail he was on now wasn't well marked, and all he had for shelter was a small, flimsy tarp.

I turned to *Yogi's PCT Handbook,* with its invaluable comments from previous hikers. "DO NOT take the old alternate route to Woody Pass . . . " Special Agent said. Teatree added, "Whatever you do, don't take this abandoned trail. . . . Unless you want to DIE on your very last day of hiking, suck it up and hike your ass . . . on the official PCT."

When did my excitement that Porter was coming home tip into terror that he wouldn't? I jumped when the phone rang. Calls to our home phone were being forwarded to my mother's. "Porter has been awarded the Texas Champion in End-of-Life Care Award," a disembodied voice said.

Would I be his widow, accepting it for him in front of hundreds of his colleagues?

Hours later, the phone rang again.

"Sweetheart," Porter said.

"You're alive."

"Of course I'm alive. But my feet are killing me. Yesterday I slipped on a wet log and fell butt-first into a deep muddy creek, but I'm great."

"Where are you?"

"In Canada. In the dining room at the Manning Park Lodge."

It was Porter all right. Food.

"I raced seventy-two miles in two and a half days. I speed-hobbled to this pay phone."

"You did it!" I sounded like an idiot.

"*We* did," he said. "In five months and ten days. I signed the trail register 'Porter-and-Gail Storey.'"

He was forty-fifth of the sixty thru-hikers who would sign the trail register at the finish, of about three hundred who'd started at the Mexican border that spring.

"Are Tom and Sheila still on the trail?" I asked. "Are they okay?"

"Suffice it to say, Sheila lost her fifty pounds, and Tom his thirty. They're not that far behind me—they'll make it. I'll call you back later, here's my salmon and gingerbread for dinner."

"Go eat before it gets cold—"

"Love you!" he said and hung up.

I love you too, I said, to Porter, myself, and everyone I knew, ever have, or ever will.

After the memorial service for my mother the next afternoon, I walked the few miles back to her apartment alone, on the nature path she walked so often. It was the same path I'd been walking when I decided to hike the Pacific Crest Trail, and when I had understood my mother was dying. It was spring then, and flowers were growing from winter's rotting wood.

Now, in autumn, leaves let go of bony branches, flew red and orange through the blue sky. What happened out there, on the trail? I struggled until I was taken by the intimate vastness of nature, just as my mother had been. I never much cared for nature, but nature cares for us.

APPENDIX A: OUR GEAR

We wore most of our clothes and gear or carried them. Our hiking outfits were almost identical: RailRiders khaki pants, Patagonia Aerius long-sleeved shirts, polyester underwear, wool/polyester socks, New Balance running shoes, and wide-brimmed sunhats. The sun was so strong, we covered our hands with white cotton gardening gloves, our necks with neckerchiefs dampened with water. In addition to our packs, we each carried a pair of light-weight carbon fiber trekking poles.

MY PACK weighed eleven pounds plus food and water, and included the following gear:

» Sleeping pad (Ridgerest closed-cell foam, cut in two pieces, each rolled into a cylinder to form a frame inside my pack and compartments for my gear)
» Down jacket (6 oz. Western Mountaineering) and attachable hood
» Raincoat with hood (Frogg Toggs with expanded nylon panel sewn in by Porter to wear over pack)
» Rainpants (GoLite)
» Montane Aero windshirt (to which Porter sewed a net hood and nylon mitts for mosquito protection)
» Pile shirt (warm but lightweight, 10 oz.)
» GoLite shorts (I gave up the sun protection of my long pants for knee mobility in the steeper mountains.)
» Fleece tights
» Panties (one extra pair) and pantiliners
» Socks (three extra pairs—one liner, one medium weight, one warm)
» Mesh shower slippers (for camp wear and stepping outside tarp at night, 1 oz.)
» Warm gloves
» Small comb
» Antiseptic wipes (three 7-inch squares a day for bathing)
» Camping toothbrush with paste inside handle; dental floss

- » Lip sunblock
- » Reading glasses
- » Pen and waterproof paper for journal
- » IDs and cash in waterproof pouch
- » Flashlight (Black Diamond Ion LED with headband, 1 oz.), spare battery

COMMUNITY GEAR:

- » Tarp (7.5 oz., from Backpackinglight.com) and titanium stakes
- » Qualcomm cell-satellite phone
- » MP3 player with recorded music
- » First-aid kit (almost a pound, since Porter is a doctor)
- » Sunblock, insect repellent
- » Silicon-coated nylon food bag (with breakfast food)
- » In the outside pockets of my pack, I carried:
- » Two one-liter water bags (Platypus)
- » Sunglasses (for high glare)
- » Lens cloth for glasses
- » Alcohol swipes and a few blister pads in assorted sizes
- » Two antiseptic wipes (for washing up)
- » Feminine urinary funnel (Sani-fem Freshette, 1 oz.)
- » Bandanna for wiping away tears
- » Waterproof watch
- » Compass
- » Pages torn from guidebook/maps

PORTER'S PACK weighed twelve pounds, plus most of the food and water, and included:

- » Sleeping pad (Therm-a-Rest Z) of six panels and three additional small pieces. His sleeping pad, plus a carbon-fiber rod, doubled as a frame for his G4-like pack home-sewn of Spectra cloth.
- » Down jacket (6 oz. Western Mountaineering, Flight series)
- » Rain Shield raincoat (with pack-cover sewn on by Porter)
- » Montane Aero windshirt (to which he attached a net hood and nylon gloves)

- » REI Polartec stretch pullover top
- » REI poly-mesh underwear
- » Wigwam INgenius crew socks (two pairs)
- » Hand-sewn nylon booties (0.8 oz.)
- » Toilet tissue (removed from roll to compress and save weight)
- » Camping toothbrush
- » Lip sunblock
- » Sunglasses, reading glasses
- » Pen and waterproof paper for journal
- » IDs and cash in waterproof pouch
- » Flashlight (Black Diamond Ion LED with headband, 1 oz.)
- » Watch
- » Compass
- » Maps

COMMUNITY GEAR:
- » One Feathered Friends down sleeping bag (zipped to Tyvek ground-cloth, with netting sewn to ground-cloth to cover our heads)
- » 1.3 litre Evernew Titanium Ultralight cooking pot
- » Pot cozy (homemade ¼ urethane foam duct-taped around pot, to keep food warm and fingers from burning)
- » Homemade "Sergeant Rock Ion" alcohol stove and support (hikinghq.net/sgt_stove/ion_stove.html)
- » Ethanol for stove (1–2 oz. per day), carried in two 375 ml Platypus bags (smaller than water bags to distinguish from water)
- » 6-liter water bag
- » Plastic sporks (two)
- » Small digital camera (Pentax Optio 4)
- » AM-FM radio (Sony SRF-M96, 1 oz.)
- » Silnylon food bags (with lunch and dinner food)

But when I left the trail, Porter had to take on my share of the community gear: tarp and stakes, first-aid kit, satellite phone and charger, sunblock and insect repellent, and all his food and water. By the end of his hike, he carried his two aluminum trekking poles (Exel), and his pack, now covered with hand-sewn patches, containing the following additions and substitutions for changing weather and conditions:

» Tarp (hand-sewn, wing-shaped for wind resistance, 1 lb., substituted for 7.5 oz. mini-tarp)
» Tarp stakes (eight titanium and two aluminum)
» Tyvek ground-cloth
» Marmot Helium 15-degree sleeping bag (1.75 lbs., substituted for Feathered Friends bag we'd had for the two of us)
» WindPro balaclava hat
» North Face boonie hat
» North Face thick pile gloves
» Wild Things Epic synthetic insulated jacket with hood (substituted for Western Mountaineering Flight jacket in wet weather)
» Patagonia Pneumatic pants
» Smartwool Aero long johns
» Ultimax crew socks (two pairs)
» Titanium spork
» Homemade gravity water filter and Pur Hiker cartridge (Jardine "Hiker's Friend," added only after Porter got sick in Northern California)
» Two dry bags (for repair materials, first-aid kit, and valuables)
» Trash compactor bags (three, to keep gear dry in pack)
» Lots of love notes from Gail

APPENDIX B: OUR FOOD

As two nutrition-conscious foodies, we packed most boxes for five days (three meals a day plus snacks), for each hundred-mile stretch of hiking at twenty miles a day. A rule of thumb was two to three pounds of (dried) food per person per day, high in oils and fats as well as proteins for added calories and taste. Our packs were heavy with food when we left each town but at least we got to eat our way through it. We felt triumphant when we came into the next town with only the little extra bit of food we'd packed in case we got stuck out there longer.

Yogi's PCT Handbook by Jackie McDonnell (trail-name "Yogi"), available through www.pcthandbook.com, is a thorough and clearly written must-have guide to planning and hiking the PCT, including notes and suggestions from previous hikers. Her excellent section on strategies for resupplying on the trail tells you what resupplies you'll find where.

Here are our suggestions for packing a resupply box, to adapt for your own needs.

First, get a sturdy cardboard carton. A standard 18x12x12-inch works well for one or two people.

Line it with a trash-compactor bag to keep out ants and moisture. The bag will also be useful on the trail, for sitting or lying on the ground. Porter laughed at me, but I found it one of my most indispensable items. My "emergency bag," we called it.

Put a scoop of laundry detergent in a plastic bag, and pack it outside the trash bag so your food doesn't smell and taste soapy.

Also outside the trash bag, we packed a one-quart metal can of denatured alcohol. (Postal regulations required a metal container, and current regulations should be checked.) One quart will be more than enough, and after you transfer what you need into your plastic alcohol bottles, you can leave the extra in the hiker box of giveaways.

To the supplies listed below, add treats too bulky to carry on the trail but nice to have when you first open your box: a can of V-8 juice, a package of cookies.

Clear a space to organize your supplies and measure into plastic bags in assorted sizes (snack, quart, and gallon are most useful). Label contents that aren't obvious (so you don't confuse sour cream powder for dry milk in the dark).

BREAKFAST:
» Instant coffee, hot chocolate, chai, teabags
» Dry milk

» Granola (¼ lb. per person/day), with variety of cereals, grains, and fruits
» Cereal bars, for variety and as alternative to granola

SNACKS AND LUNCH:
» Nuts (1 lb. per five-day box), salty and oily for more calories, e.g., cashews, almonds, honey-roasted peanuts
» Peanut butter
» Party mix (one bag), mixed chips and pretzels, etc.
» Dried fruit (one bag), the more dehydrated the lighter in weight
» Energy bars (two per person per day)
» Chocolate bars (two per person per day); dark chocolate doesn't melt as quickly as milk chocolate
» Jerky (4-oz. bag), beef or turkey, in variety of seasonings
» Kippers (one can per day)
» Tuna (one 3-oz. foil packet per day), in a variety of seasonings
» Crackers or cocktail rye

DINNERS:
» Pastas and noodles including ramen, couscous, instant rice, mashed potatoes, as well as boxed combinations like macaroni and cheese
» Dehydrated beans, beef, chicken, turkey, tofu, texturized vegetable protein
» Dried vegetables such as peas, tomatoes, corn, carrots, green peppers
» Soup packets
» Seasoning packets in a variety of flavors: Thai, Italian, pizza, spaghetti, pesto, taco, beef stroganoff, salsa, etc., as well as spices such as dried minced garlic and curry
» Parmesan cheese (brick or powdered lasts longer); powders made from sour cream, spinach, tomatoes
» Olive oil (4- or 8-oz. bottle)

How to cook a one-pot dinner with a balance of protein, carbohydrates, and fats in a 3-oz. pot (1.3 liters):

To three cups of water in a pot, add dried vegetables, meat, or protein, and one ounce of olive oil. Bring to a boil, stir in carbohydrate (pasta, potatoes, or instant rice, etc.). After reaching a second boil, stir in seasoning or soup packet. Remove from heat, cover, and put pot in a cozy. (Porter made the cozy to insulate our pot with a piece of closed-cell foam pad. See zenstoves.net /PotAccessories.htm#BuildaPotCozy.) Let cook in a hot covered pot (off stove to save fuel and keep from burning) for fifteen to twenty minutes.

When the food is ready to eat, garnish it with a powder such as sour cream or Parmesan cheese.

In bear country, take great precautions to protect your food, beyond hanging it from a tree limb. Bears have such a keen sense of smell, they can detect cooking odors on your gear even if you hike further down the trail after dinner. The National Park Service advises, and in some areas requires, hikers to carry their food in personal bear-proof canisters (Bearikade Expedition, www.wild-ideas.net). Porter gallantly carried one large enough (2 lbs. and 6 oz. empty and 30 lbs. full) for all of our food, and substituted items such as less-bulky couscous for noodles to pack it all in. Still, we had to resort to self-rising flour or complete cake mixes (flavored with food powders such as cheese, spinach, tomato, cinnamon) to make dough and bake nutritious breads.

An ultralight 4-oz. BakePacker can be purchased to bake in the wilderness, but you can make a 1½-oz. one yourself, as Porter did. First, make a steamer from a heavy foil basting pan or pie plate (available at grocery stores), by cutting four strips from it one inch wide and the length of the pan's diameter, and stapling these together in the middle. Bend the strips open so they radiate out from the center staple evenly. Put this stapled steamer in the base of your cooking pot.

How to bake filling, doughy breads in your steamer/baker:

Put water in the pot almost to the top of the steamer (or Bake-Packer).

To make dough: in a plastic bag, add enough water to your flavored self-rising flour or complete cake mix to make a stiff dough. Knead for several minutes, then put dough (still in plastic bag) on top of the steamer in the pot. Cover. Boil twenty minutes (about when fuel is used up), and put the pot in the cozy for ten more minutes to continue baking. Open the plastic bag, put the pot lid into the bag on top of the dough, turn it over, and peel off the plastic bag.

Porter's cheese breads and cinnamon breads baked on the trail proved to be wonderful comfort food, particularly served with hot chai or tea as the sun was going down.

Other items to pack in your resupply box (or in a 5-gallon paint can "float bucket" to mail ahead from post office to post office as you progress up the trail):

» Guidebook pages (including maps) for the section you'll be hiking with these supplies
» Journal paper (we used Rite in the Rain all-weather writing paper, www.riteintherain.com or 253-922-5000)
» Stamped, self-addressed envelope to mail completed journal pages home
» Ballpoint pens (two)
» Batteries for your flashlight, camera, radio, or MP3 player (or recharger if you're using an iPod)
» Travel-size toothpaste and dental floss
» Antiseptic wipes (three per person per day for hygiene) and small quantity of toilet tissue
» Lens cloths for your glasses (one per day)
» Vitamins, medications
» First-aid resupplies such as blister pads (Band-Aid Activ-Flex bandages) and ibuprofen (called "vitamin I" on the trail)

Instead of packing one box at a time, it's more efficient to pack them on an assembly line. First, study the guidebooks (e.g., *Yogi's PCT Handbook* by Jackie McDonnell, and Leslie C. Croot's *Pacific Crest Trail Town Guide* published by the Pacific Crest Trail Association) to figure out where you want to ship each box, based on your estimated daily mileage and the distance between towns. Some mail drops will be in towns where you have a choice between the post office (c/o General Delivery) and motels that hold hiker packages. The post office has limited hours, and you might not want to wait all weekend for it to open on Monday if you can stay at a motel. Some motels accept packages sent through the United States Postal Service (Priority Mail works best), others only those sent UPS. If there's any doubt, call first, even to find out whether the post office or motel is still there.

Address each box with its destination and your return address, and in the lower left corner, print "Please hold for PCT hiker, ETA _____" (your estimated date of arrival).

Line up your boxes in the order in which they'll be shipped. Note how many days of food to pack for each box on one of the flaps. Make a shopping list. Order some items (e.g., dehydrated meats, fruits, veggies) from online sources (e.g., www.justtomatoes.com). Buy what you can at wholesale hypermarkets, and the rest from supermarkets and health food stores. So you don't get bored eating the same things over and over, buy as much of a variety of flavors and brands as possible, especially for energy bars, candy bars, nuts, sauce packets, and pastas.

Ideally, you'll have someone at home who'll shop for additional items while you're hiking, based on your latest list of food cravings. Leave your boxes unsealed for any additional items your resupply person will need to include at the last minute: gear you request, any mail you need to see or handle, and perishable food like bread and apples.

Once taped securely, have your boxes shipped off in plenty of time to arrive at remote destinations. Thank your resupply person effusively and often.

APPENDIX C: EMERGENCY LISTS

I compiled two lists, the first our financial and insurance information to help our families dispose of our estates, in the unlikely event we died on the trail. The other was our list of vital contact numbers we'd need to keep our life going while on the trail, condensed and printed onto one sheet of waterproof paper. If you make one of your own, organize and abbreviate the information so it's clear to you but not an identity thief. At the risk of being as compulsive as Benjamin Franklin, here's what to include:

» Your own phone numbers (home, cell, satellite) and codes to retrieve your messages
» Long-distance calling card and customer service numbers
» Bank and credit card account numbers with customer service phone numbers in case of loss
» Insurance company phone and policy numbers for health and property
» Physician, dentist, psychotherapist, and attorney phone numbers
» "In case of emergency, please contact" phone numbers (this in bold caps)
» Family and friends' phone numbers and addresses (for those you might want to contact during your trip)
» Business and government phone numbers you might need (e.g., 800 numbers for your gear suppliers, the Pacific Crest Trail Association, ranger stations)

You'd be surprised how helpful such a list is, not to mention you'll forget your own phone number when wilderness survival takes up all your psychic space.

I PROMISE NOT TO SUFFER

AN INTERVIEW WITH AUTHOR GAIL D. STOREY IN THREE PARTS

The Pacific Crest Trail (PCT) is 2,663 miles long, stretching from Mexico to Canada, and is considered one of the world's great hiking routes and an immense physical challenge. Prior to beginning this hike, author Gail D. Storey had participated in a few long-distance cycling trips but had virtually no hiking or backpacking experience. Or, as she puts it at the beginning of her book *I Promise Not to Suffer: A Fool for Love Hikes the Pacific Crest Trail*, "I never much cared for nature, or rather, thought it okay as long as it stayed outside."

Mountaineers Books editor in chief Kate Rogers sat down with Gail to ask about her book and the adventure it describes, covering some of the many questions and comments we've heard from a wide variety of readers over the past year.

THE PCT AND HIKING ADVENTURE

Q *As the book unfolds, you write that you couldn't bear the thought of being parted from your husband Porter for months while he attempted this trail—and so you hiked. Was it really that simple? Was there anything else that drove you to take on this audacious adventure? What do you think might inspire other women to hit the trail?*

A No, it wasn't that simple. Initially, I was drawn by my love for Porter, both wanting to be with him and not wanting to drive myself crazy with worry while he hiked the trail. But then I began to wonder what drew him so obsessively to the wilderness, not to mention to living and hiking out there for months. To hike the PCT was neither an impulsive nor a practical decision; it wasn't really a decision at all. It was based on an inner knowing; there was an inevitability to it, one of those moments when Life says: "This is what wants to happen, and it will, so you're better off surrendering."

The women I've spoken with have many different reasons—athletic, emotional, spiritual—to hike the trail, but underneath them I sense a deep longing for the earth itself, as a living, breathing being. Women have a powerful, intuitive affinity for the earth.

Q *You and Porter meet some wonderful fellow hikers on the PCT. Why do you think you and Sheila bonded so immediately?*

A Sheila and I recognized each other immediately by the courage we sensed in each other behind our deer-in-the-headlights shock that we were out there. We'd survived a terrifying storm two nights before, Tom and Sheila up on the mountain, and Porter and I descending to the base of the mountain. I think what we felt for each other was instant compassion and respect.

Q *The PCT's "trail angels" play a key role in helping hikers along the route. Why do you think these folks volunteer and dedicate themselves so completely to a bunch of stinky hikers just passing through? Which of the angels was most significant during your journey?*

A Not to get all woo-woo about it, but I feel they're called trail "angels" with good cause, in that they're imbued with kindness and love. You can feel it in their presence, whether they're picking you up at a trailhead, serving you tacos or pancakes, or driving you to the doctor. Many trail angels have hiked all or part of the trail themselves, and they truly understand how raw and vulnerable you're likely to be. In addition to the legendary trail angels Donna and Jeff Saufley and Terrie and Joe Anderson, those who lugged gallons of water to remote caches in the Southern California desert saved us from nearly dying of dehydration. The relationship between trail angels and thru-hikers is a lovefest of generosity and gratitude.

Q *Much, if not all, of your hiking gear was highly specialized, ultra lightweight, and handmade (or adapted) by Porter. Distance hikers are notoriously fascinated by this stuff, but what do you think was behind Porter's desire (obsession?) to make all your gear?*

A Two fundamental elements of Porter's nature go into his making our ultralight gear: his extraordinarily inventive mind and his desire to be a great provider. While I wake up at night with what I call my "3 a.m. remorse" for oversharing at a dinner party (!), Porter wakes up with a design for a heretofore-unimagined wilderness baking apparatus or backpack or tarp. Also, he's determined to take as good care of me in the wilderness as I take of him at home. He has the virtues of a caveman when it comes to the primal need to provide food and shelter for the family, both at home and in the wild.

Q *Ultimately, after about two and a half months and 900 miles, you have to leave the trail, primarily due to your loss of weight. You write that just before you leave, you "felt inseparable now from the vast green and blue and white of the wilderness." For a gal who never much cared for nature, what did you mean?*

A It was the closest I've come to a dissolution of the small self into oneness with our essential nature. Even to say tree and sky and snow would have felt excessively definitive of a subject (me)–object (the world) relationship. Rather, the natural world and I within it came and went—effortlessly, exquisitely—in the spacious oneness.

Q *There have been a number of books recently about the PCT, such as* Wild *by Cheryl Strayed,* The Cactus Eaters *by Dan White, and others. What do you think draws writers to the trail? How is your book different—and how is it the same—as these other PCT adventures?*

A What I most appreciate about these books—and many classics about journeys from *The Odyssey* to Peter Matthiessen's *The Snow Leopard*—is how the journey is a metaphor for life. As Joseph Campbell articulated so well in his book *The Hero with a Thousand Faces*, the mythic journey is one of departure, initiation, and return with a boon for the community. Writers are drawn to so organic a story structure as a journey of transformation.

However, I'm even more deeply drawn to the non-linear journey, the spiral structure of story as a descent into psychological, psychosexual, and psychospiritual underworlds. Maureen Murdock's book *The Heroine's Journey* delves deeply into woman's quest for wholeness. The physical adventure of hiking the PCT aroused emotional resonances with my past, family, life with Porter, and spirituality that interwove themselves quite naturally into the story.

I'm fascinated by how complementary Cheryl Strayed's brilliant book *Wild* and mine are. Cheryl was twenty-six when she hiked the PCT, I was fifty-six. She hiked solo, I hiked with my husband of seventeen years. Our relationships with our mothers were pivotal to our experiences on the trail, with her mother dying beforehand and mine at the end. Yet each of our books seems to be the story of the heroine's journey, a descent into the core of our being and a yearning to reconnect with the deep feminine.

MARRIAGE AND THE LOVE STORY

Q *Hiking the Pacific Crest Trail was a sort of vision quest for your husband Porter, a way to deal with his midlife crisis and career upheaval. You, in turn, chose to upend your own life in order to help him achieve this dream. Is it a realistic expectation for one half of a couple to go to such extremes for the other, when the dream in question is so personal and, in many ways, a type of indulgence?*

A My mother once told me that in a marriage, each person has to give 200 percent. It startled me because her own marriage was so hard, although I understand now that my mother and father each did the best they possibly could given what life had dealt them. I absorbed the essence of her statement, though— that we don't dole out only so much love and that's that. Another couple might find an entirely different way of helping each other achieve a dream, or leave each other to their own devices. It's not about what extremes we go to or don't go to for the other person, but about our actions coming from love. The wonderful paradox is that in a relationship grounded in love, each person feels the abundance.

Q *Not many couples could survive the kind of intense one-on-one time together that you and Porter faced—you often fought with each other, and at times he seemed to want you to leave. How did you manage it?*

A We were amazed at our ability to put up with each other! It was an evolving thing, in that we each had to learn the many different ways to cut each other slack as the need arose. I learned to not take everything personally. I'm a very expressive person; I never met an emotion I didn't like. Porter has a lot of empathy and compassion, well developed through his work as a hospice and palliative care physician. My heart went out to him when he was having a hard time, as his did to me.

Q *You continued to support Porter from afar after you left the trail, and at the end of the hike your relationship with him seems stronger. But is it? Or, in fact, was the relationship completely altered by this adventure, rearranged into something wholly new?*

A Porter and I had each been doing our inner work, individually and as a couple, before and throughout our marriage. Our hike was a practice ground for everything we'd learned up to that point. Living outside for months, completely removed from our previous day-to-day lives, we learned to trust each other in ways that crises allow. So yes, in addition to the deepened trust in ourselves and each other, our relationship was subsumed by trust itself in nature, life, and love.

Q *This book is in many ways about what you learned while on your husband's big life adventure. Do you have an adventure or dream of your own that Porter, in his turn, has or will go all out to support in the same way as you did for him?*

A What comes immediately to mind is how supportive Porter has been and continues to be throughout the writing and publication of *I Promise Not to Suffer*, and as we make it widely available to readers. He vetted the manuscript for truth and clarity, encouraged me when I despaired, and took on more than his share of the household tasks. He arranges his own work schedule to accompany me on book events across the country, is my driver and IT guy, even participates in radio interviews when the host asks. I call him my "full-service author escort"! He's with me every step of the way.

INNERLIFE AND SPIRITUAL ADVENTURE

Q *In the book, you write, "I was learning that pain wasn't the same as suffering—I could hurt and still be okay." Given the title of your book, can you explain what you mean?*

A My habitual defenses against pain—physical, emotional, and spiritual—didn't work in so exposed an environment as the Pacific Crest Trail. Arguing with pain only increased the suffering. When we don't resist it, pain is simply a sensation, one of many in the ever-shifting flow of our experiences. No matter how much I hurt, deep within I was fine. That astonished me. Rather than anesthetizing myself against pain or any experience, I felt whatever was happening with more color, texture, and aliveness. Free in that spaciousness, I could take care of any pain from a deeper intelligence.

So when Porter expressed his concern for me going into the High Sierra by saying he hated to see me suffer, I could say in all honesty, "I promise not to suffer." It was funny, but also true.

Q *Your mother died shortly after you left the trail and, in the book, you describe how you at last found peace in your relationship with her. How did your experiences on the PCT play a role in that newfound understanding?*

A The earth is truly our mother, and I was nurtured on the trail by her fiercely compassionate love. I came to know that love is the essence of our being, and that I had felt it all along through my own mother's love.

Q *After an argument with Porter, you run ahead on the trail and, rounding a curve, almost run smack into a mountain lion. This encounter is brief; the lion slips away and you write,*

"In the absolute quiet, everything was light and clear. The mountains fell away. All there was was the loveliness of silence. I existed to listen. I was the listening." It's clearly a powerful moment. But my heart would have been racing! Why do you think the encounter allowed you to feel such quiet and stillness?

A The benevolent power of our meeting, one being to another, rocketed me out my mind and body as a separate self. Form and matter felt insubstantial and illusory, even the mountains clattered down like a stage set. Was it a direct connection with the "I am"? I had been holding the question "Who am I?", or it was holding me, and it drew me right into that rich, full, vibrant silence, with nothing to do but ring with open listening.

Q *Your summer hiking adventure is now several years in the past. How did hiking the PCT transform you as an individual? What experiences from the trail have you carried over into your daily life? Do you live your life differently now because of that hike?*

A Our lives changed radically after we hiked the PCT. We moved to Boulder, Colorado, where we gutted an old house down to the studs and rebuilt it according to green values with solar and photovoltaic energy, in a meadow of native trees and plants. We bike and hike wherever we can; our one car mostly sits in the garage. Our love affair is constantly evolving to meet the needs of our work and our responsibilities to the community, local and global. We try to live consciously from the mystery and inherent lovability within us all.

Once you're taken up by mystery, you can never go back. No back to go back to. It's all in the right now. What Porter and I might call our lives flows out of that luminosity. Everything's included. Terrible and beautiful things have happened since our hike, but it would be tragic not to go along with life's cosmic sense of humor. And we keep walking deeper and deeper, as we did on the trail, into the question "Who am I?"

QUESTIONS AND TOPICS FOR GROUP DISCUSSION

1 Gail D. Storey, author of *I Promise Not to Suffer: A Fool for Love Hikes the Pacific Crest Trail*, has had a tremendous response from readers who connect with her experiences on the trail, in her marriage, and of coming to terms with herself. As a reader, what has been your response to *I Promise Not to Suffer*? What is your favorite episode in the book?

2 What do you think Gail meant by "No, no, no! But yes," in deciding to hike the Pacific Crest Trail with Porter? Have you ever gone ahead with something for reasons you didn't understand? To what lengths would you go to help someone you love fulfill a dream?

3 Was it foolhardy or brave for the couple to sell their house, car, and many of their possessions to simplify their lives and to finance their adventure? What do you make of the seemingly opposite ways Gail and Porter prepared for the trail?

4 Porter and Gail had been married for seventeen years when they hiked the Pacific Crest Trail. Would you set out on a journey that basically throws you together 24/7 with your partner or spouse?

5 Gail and Porter bonded with Sheila and Tom, despite differences in their ages, family backgrounds, careers, and preparation for the hike. Have you made friends in unlikely circumstances, because of something you went through together?

6 Do you feel the sexual relationship shown between Gail and Porter is typical or unusual? Did Gail's frankness on the topic inspire you or embarrass you?

7 The first dangerous storm; an injury, such as Porter's foot fracture or Gail's torn shoulder muscle; dehydration in the high desert; freezing cold in the High Sierra; Gail's near-drowning in the rapids; her dangerous weight loss—what crisis do you think would have driven you off the trail?

8 Have you ever had an experience of such complete stillness and silence like the one Gail writes about when she met the mountain lion? What were the circumstances?

9 Do you find that the other dimensions of Gail and Porter's lives, interwoven into the story of the hike, distract from or deepen the narrative?

10 Gail's relationship with her mother was complex. Being with her mother when she died, Gail experienced a profound healing of that relationship. Can you relate to the strains in their bond, in regard to your own mother or father or perhaps a child? Have you found such resolution with someone ill or dying?

11 Hiking the Pacific Crest Trail transformed Gail and Porter individually and as a couple. What outdoor adventures or other experiences have transformed you—physically, emotionally, and/or spiritually?

ABOUT THE AUTHOR

Gail D. Storey is the author of the novels *The Lord's Motel* (called by the *New York Times* Book Review "a tale of unwise judgments and wise humor") and its sequel, *God's Country Club* (a Barnes & Noble Discover Great New Writers Selection), as well as stories, essays, and articles in magazines. Gail's blog at gailstorey.com features photos and videos related to *I Promise Not to Suffer: A Fool for Love Hikes the Pacific Crest Trail*, including ultra-light gear for the journey through the dark night of the wilderness into unconditional happiness. Her blog at amberstorey.com pokes soulful fun at pretty much everything. A proficient hoopdancer and trans-American tandem bicyclist, she is also notorious for jumping out of cakes, as seen on her YouTube channel, GailStorey. She lives in Boulder, Colorado, with her long-suffering husband, Porter Storey, MD FACP FAAHPM, a national leader in hospice and palliative medicine.

THE BARBARA SAVAGE
MILES FROM NOWHERE
MEMORIAL AWARD

The Barbara Savage *Miles From Nowhere* Memorial Award commemorates the late Barbara Savage, author of the bestselling book *Miles From Nowhere: A Round-the-World Bicycle Adventure*, published in 1983. Tragically, Barbara was killed in a cycling accident shortly before the book's publication. The author's husband, Larry Savage, created an award fund in cooperation with The Mountaineers Books by donating the royalties from Barbara's book to encourage personal adventure and writing in the same spirit as *Miles From Nowhere*.

Barbara Savage Award winners are compelling accounts of personal journeys, typically experienced through a muscle-powered outdoor adventure, that vividly convey a sense of the risks, joys, hardships, triumphs, humor, and accidents of fate that are inevitably part of any such journey.

Barbara Savage *Miles From Nowhere* Memorial Award titles include:

» *Himalayan Passage: Seven Months in the High Country of Tibet, Nepal, China, India, and Pakistan,* by Jeremy Schmidt

» *Where the Pavement Ends: One Woman's Bicycle Trip Through Mongolia, China, and Vietnam,* by Erika Warmbrunn

» *Spirited Waters: Soloing South Through the Inside Passage,* by Jennifer Hahn

» *A Blistered Kind of Love: One Couple's Trial by Trail,* by Angela and Duffy Ballard

» *Faith of Cranes: Finding Hope and Family in Alaska,* by Hank Lentfer

» *I Promise Not to Suffer: A Fool for Love Hikes the Pacific Crest Trail,* by Gail D. Storey

OTHER MOUNTAINEERS BOOKS YOU MIGHT ENJOY

Miles from Nowhere: A Round-the-World Bicycle Adventure *Barbara Savage*
A funny, honest, and poignant account of the Savages' two-year, 23,000 mile, 25-country around-the-world cycling tour.

Pacific Crest Trailside Reader, California: Adventure, History, and Legend on the Long Distance Trail *Edited by Rees Hughes and Corry Lewis*

Pacific Crest Trailside Reader, Oregon and Washington: Adventure, History, and Legend on the Long Distance Trail *Edited by Rees Hughes and Corry Lewis*
Stories to delight the imaginations of everyone who has hiked, will hike, or dreams of hiking the world's most beautiful walk in the woods.

The Bar Mitzvah and the Beast: One Family's Cross-Country Ride of Passage by Bike *Matt Biers-Ariel*
"Man plans, God laughs" (old Jewish saying). You'll fall in love with this family on their cross-country bike trip, meant to replace the traditional Jewish bar mitzvah for their thirteen-year-old son.

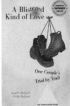

A Blistered Kind of Love: One Couple's Trial by Trail *Angela and Duffy Ballard*
A young couple's story of the epic Pacific Crest Trail adventure that deepened their bond—or did it?

Spirited Waters: Soloing South Through the Inside Passage *Jennifer Hahn*
A gripping account of one woman's unforgettable and challenging kayaking journey.

The Mountaineers Books has more than 500 outdoor recreation titles in print.
For more details visit
www.mountaineersbooks.org.